I should like to pay particular thanks to my brother in law Graeme Jenner for his great help in "fine tuning" this book. He is married to my sister Wendy and they live in Iver, quite near to where Ken and Yvonne Price lived, so he knew them both well. This has helped give me personal insights into Ken's life in post war Iver.

Profits from the sale of this book are being donated to the RAF Benevolent Fund , who rely on these funds to support past and present RAF personnel. By purchasing this book you have helped towards this vital work.

KENNETH GEORGE PRICE
DFC AND BAR

- his part in the Great Escape from Stalag Luft III in 1944 -
Alistair Price

Published by
Alistair R Price

Printed by
Creative Design and Print Solutions Ltd
Alveston House,
11 Broad Street
Pershore,
Worcs WR10 1BB

A Tribute to the life of
Kenneth George Price DFC
by
Alistair Price

Alistair P

CONTENTS

CHAPTER 1

Introduction

Dear Reader, I hope you will forgive my indulgence in writing a book about my father, Kenneth Price. I realise that many of us will have fathers with their own story to tell about their time during WW2 but I am very proud of mine. He came from a relatively poor background and join the RAF, rising up through the ranks as an officer and on his demobilisation, in April 1946 had risen to the rank of Wing Commander. He played a part as one of the famous "Pathfinders" in Bomber Command completing 58 "trips" (missions), before being shot down in July 1943. Having been captured, he then spent nearly two years as a prisoner of war in Stalag Luft 111, Poland, took part in the Great Escape and the subsequent notorious "Long March".

My father's experience was extraordinary and this story is an important part of his life and a history of the period.

CHAPTER 2

Kenneth's early years

Kenneth and his identical twin brother, Douglas, were born on 4th October 1919 to parents George and Harriet Price at their home in Swan Lane, Coventry. Ken and Doug were not the first born, as they had an elder sister who was born on 16th April 1916, and sadly lived only for three weeks. On 8th October 1920, the family however, celebrated the arrival of their younger sister Peggy, to whom the boys were completed devoted all their lives.

Ken's father was in and out of work for most of his life. Rejected by the Army in 1915 due to foot problems, he took a job in a munitions factory, which he hated. Just after the end of the First World War (WW1), he took a corner shop selling general groceries in Stoney Stanton Road, Coventry, which sadly wasn't successful. He then took a stall in Coventry market in 1921, where the two boys played and got under his feet.

KEN AND DOUGLAS UNDER 18 TABLE TENNIS CHAMPIONS

Not much is known about Ken's early years, but he must have been quite bright as at the age of 13 he won a scholarship to King Henry V111 grammar school in Coventry. Ken matriculated (which in the thirties was similar to A levels now) and gained credits in English and History. Both Ken and Doug were very good table tennis players – becoming under 18 table tennis champions of Warwickshire.

Like his father, Ken was good at English and on leaving school in 1937 got a job as a reporter on the Midland Daily Telegraph (subsequently renamed the Coventry Evening Telegraph). He was only employed at the paper for two years, and received many accolades about his style of writing and reporting.

In 1938, Ken foresaw that war was imminent and rather than being pushed into a service (i.e. Army, Navy or Air Force) chosen for him, he decided to enroll part time in the Royal Air Force Volunteer Reserve (RAFVR) at Ansty near Coventry. Ansty had a long runway, which throughout the Second World War (WW2) could accommodate heavy bombers – that required long runways to take off with their bomb loads. Ken had a great interest in flying - most people who joined up wanted to serve as pilots, but Ken opted for the navigation role instead, as he loved maps and meteorology (put simply, the study of the weather).

CHAPTER 3

Called up to join the RAF

Ken received his call up papers to join the RAF on 1st September 1939, at the age of 20. After training he was posted to Catterick in Yorkshire where he flew in night fighters between February and September 1940. He took part in the Battle of Britain, flying in Fairey Battles and Bristol Blenheims which were notoriously slow and certainly no match for the Messerschmitt 109 fighters of the German Luftwaffe. These British aircraft were developed in the mid 1930s but were based on older airframes such as the Hawker Hart and Hind biplanes from WW1 and were hopelessly outclassed.

In 1941, he was posted to Bomber Command and gained experience in a number of aircraft – once again flying Fairey Battles (which could only accommodate a small bomb load); Handley Page Hampdens – twin engine bombers powered by Pegasus or Perseus radial engines which had a maximum speed of 247 mph – still much slower than the ME 109 from the Luftwaffe (348 mph); Avro Manchesters – another twin engine bomber powered by Vulture engines but extremely underpowered for the airframe, with a maximum speed of 265 mph; and then to the Lancaster, the most famous of all WW2 bombers, developed by Avro's Roy Chadwick with four Merlin engines (the engine also powered the Spitfire) that made this the most successful of all bombers in the war. They had a range of 2,530 miles and a maximum speed of 287 mph. It was well armed, and they flew over 156,000 sorties during the war.

From the very beginning of the war, the Coventry Evening Telegraph was completely supportive of their employees and by the beginning of 1941 they produced "Our Boys' News-Letter"- an article which was dedicated to all employees serving in HM Forces (all of whom could expect their jobs back at the end of hostilities). There are a few entries about both Ken & Doug and extracts are included in this book. In December 1941, the News Letter reports that Ken arrived at the paper's offices dressed in the uniform of a flying officer in the RAF. They say *"we salute you"* and that they will officially record his promotion in the next issue of "Our Boys' News-Letter" in January 1942. In the same article, the Telegraph reported that after a big raid that was badly disrupted by the weather, Doug had proposed to Joan, a young lady he had been dating. The paper then continued to remark that they wondered "how long will it be before Ken follows suit?" Actually, it wasn't until June 1945 for reasons that will become clear, that Ken got engaged to the lady who became the "love of his life" – Yvonne. After Ken and Doug joined the RAF in 1939, their identical twin status was to cause some amusing experiences – (more of which later). In June 1942, the Welfare Record (previously the "Our Boys' News-Letter") produced an interesting and amusing insight on the boys. Headed "Those Twins" – it says:

"It would not surprise us to hear that the High Command had banned the recruiting of twins especially in the same service. The Brothers Price must have caused the administrative section of the RAF quite a lot of work and many a WAAF has no doubt left the office after a day's "watch" wondering why the twins were born at all. Not long ago Doug – (or was it Ken?) called in to the Telegraph offices at Nuneaton and related the story of how he had his brother's number, and his brother had his! After two years the RAF had discovered that according to their records, "Doug" was "Ken" and "Ken" was "Doug". That could not be, so they had to change numbers and all that went with it. Medical papers were altered; a tooth that had been "Ken's" for two years now belonged to "Doug", so no wonder "Ken" said it didn't ache! - it wasn't his tooth at all! Even in the little matter of income-tax forms, "Ken" was "Doug" and "Doug" was "Ken", but as both were then of equal rank and presumably received equal pay, it is doubtful if much harm was done. Now one of them – "Ken" has a commission, but "Doug" may have received his by the time this appears and so the twin personalities will continue."

n the Ledgers

is represented in all three Services, in widely separated theatres of as, and in the air. Lance-Corporal he Department in the Middle East, two colleagues from other sections.

Institute of Secretaries. He is now in training in the R.A.F.V.R. as a pilot.

"Our Twins!"

"DOUG.," of the famous Price twins, came to Nuneaton the other day. He and his brother "Ken." were in that big raid when the weather so tragically upset calculations, and we were glad to know they both "weathered the storm." The twins are now cadets awaiting commissions. Good luck to them! "The engagement is announced . . ." Congratulations, "Doug." How long will "Ken." be before he follows suit?

As the "News-Letter" stonehand was about to put the above matter in the forme, a telephone message was received from our special correspondent at Coventry, saying that "Ken" had arrived at the Hertford Street office. He was wearing the uniform of a Flying-Officer. We salute you, "Ken." The promotion will be officially recorded in our next issue.

Corporal Newbold writes from Taunton to say he is "a true countryman, with a daily round that includes feeding the fowl and the ducks!" He adds. "I get the 'Telegraph' regularly, and pass it round to five other Coventry exiles down here."

OUR BOYS NEWS-LETTER DECEMBER 1941

which, he said, reminded him of the Office games.

"Bob" Croft. — Let's hear from you, Bob, for it seems years since we had a line.

Those Twins!

● **IT WOULD NOT SURPRISE US** to hear that the High Command had banned the recruiting of twins, especially in the same Service. The **Brothers Price** must have caused the administrative section of the R.A.F. quite a lot of work, and many a W.A.A.F. has, no doubt, left the office after a day's "watch," wondering why twins were born at all.

Not long ago, "Doug."—or was it "Ken."?—called in the offices at Nuneaton and related the story of how he had his brother's number, and his brother had his! After two years, the R.A.F. had discovered that, according to their records, "Doug." was "Ken.," and "Ken." was "Doug." That could not be; so they had to change numbers and all that went with it. Medical papers were altered; a tooth that had been "Ken's" for two years now belonged to "Doug."—no wonder "Ken." said it didn't ache! Of course, it wasn't his tooth at all!

Even in the little matter of income-tax forms, "Ken." was "Doug.," and "Doug." was "Ken.," but as both were then of equal rank and presumably received equal pay, it is doubtful if very much harm was done. Now one of them—"Ken."—has a commission, but "Doug." may have received his by the time this appears, and so the twin personalities will continue.

and Star," is now in that Tank Regiment in the Middle East, and, according to his latest letter, "still going strong."

WELFARE RECORD JUNE 1942

KEN & DOUG IN UNIFORM IN 1943

It is worth recording that Ken flew in no fewer than fourteen types of aircraft before he was shot down. The first record in his logbook shows he spent 40 minutes in an Avro Anson on 30th July 1939, which was a twin engine multi role aircraft and was his first flight after joining the RAFVR.

He actually flew in the following aircraft (in date order):

- **Fairey Battle January 1940** - single engine light bomber that was also used as a night fighter, but was no match for the ME109 fighter from the Luftwaffe.
- **Handley Page Harrow 1940** - a slow twin engine bomber

- **Hawker Demon 1940** - two seat biplane and fighter in which he spent much time on gunnery practice.
- **Westland Wallace 1940** - two seat general purpose biplane, where he spent time training on cameras and photographing targets on the ground.
- **Bristol Blenheim 1940** - twin engine light bomber used extensively in the first two years of the war. In April 1940, he was posted to Guernsey where he was patrolling in a Blenheim when it was engaged by a ME109. They escaped safely. Much of the time was spent in covering Allied troops on the Cherbourg peninsular. In October and November of that year he was involved in bombing German invasion barges at Boulogne and Calais.
- **Vickers Wellington December 1940** - twin engine long range bomber.
- **Avro Manchester – January 1941** - twin engine medium bomber. It was slow, but could carry bomb loads to the heart of Germany – e.g. Hamburg in March.
- **Handley Page Hampden July 1941** - twin engine medium bomber.
- **Avro Lancaster February 1942** - This was his first trip in this four engine bomber. On a trip back from Germany in May, they shot up a night fighter.
- **Miles Mentor August 1942** - single engine training and communications aircraft used for flights between UK air bases.
- **Lysander October 1942** - Single engine liaison aircraft, which had an amazing short field and landing ability, that was used in many operations in support of the French resistance.

- **Short Sterling August 1943** – first four engine bomber to be brought into service in Bomber Command.
- **De Haviland Mosquito 27th July 1943** – his only flight in this aircraft and he was shot down returning from a trip to Duisburg over Holland.

During his RAF service Ken spent a total of 589 hours flying time, of which 225 were at night.

Ken was posted to 83 Squadron at Wyton in Huntingdonshire on 17th August 1942 where he was part of the newly formed Pathfinders. Pathfinders were the brainchild of Air Vice-Marshall Don Bennett, a very strong-willed New Zealander. Their role was to set course and drop "marker" flares over the targets so that the bomber formations would have something to aim at. In the early stages of the war, many bomb loads missed their targets and the Pathfinders were able to give the bomber crews a better chance of locating the actual target. Another result was to stop "creep back" where crews dropped bombloads early. The Pathfinders were extremely successful in stopping this and improving accuracy, as will be seen later.

Ken's operations included such places as Hamburg (5 hour round trip), Dusseldorf, Kiel, Brest, Wanderdog in Saxony, Bremen, Saarbrucken, Genoa, Lorient, St Nazaire, Cologne , Montchanin (6 hours 25 minutes round trip), Turin (10 hours round trip), Duisburg and Essen on 25th July 1943, when they had General Arnold of the USAAF on board.

These operations were interspersed with on-going training, including the increased use of radar, wireless communications and formation flying. Bombers flying together, in formation, gave much greater protection against night fighters.

In December 1942, the Welfare Record reports that Ken was promoted to Flight Lieutenant and in June 1943 was promoted to Squadron Leader and became the Wyton Station Navigation Officer. He was also the Station Radar Instructor and it was whilst here that he spotted a young WAAF corporal with responsibility for issuing maps to air crew. Yvonne was swinging her legs on the edge of a table and Ken was immediately attracted! Yvonne was certainly his "target for tonight!"

Ken was awarded the Distinguished Flying Cross (DFC) on 9th July 1943. The official citation remarked:

"This officer has completed many successful attacks on enemy targets. He has served in fighter and bomber aircraft, and his enthusiasm and skill have been most praiseworthy at all times. His keenness and efficiency have been largely responsible for the successes achieved by his crew. In addition to his operational duties Squadron Leader Price has also had much success in the capacity of Station Navigation Officer. His guidance and example have contributed much to the standard of navigation achieved in the unit. Squadron Leader Price's services, both on the ground and in the air, have been highly commendable."

Ken flew a total of 58 sorties and was awarded a Bar to his DFC for his leadership and gallantry. The life expectancy of a bomber crew in WW2 was just 5 trips, so Ken was lucky and far exceeded these expectations. It a little-known fact, that there was a greater rate of attrition of bomber crew in WW2, than there were officers in the trenches in WW1. 55,573 bomber crew were lost during WW2.

Many Pathfinder crew took a good luck charm with them, eg: a rear gunner might have taken his girlfriend's knickers, another pyjamas and in one known case, one of the crew even took his dog complete with its own oxygen mask in the rear turret! The family believe that Ken took the letters he received from his girlfriend Yvonne (WAAF).

In February 1944, the Air Ministry commentator said to the press that "the secret of success of all heavy raids on Germany is the Pathfinder Force. Over the past two years the RAF has built up the most highly skilled corps of flying men in the world". Pathfinder Corps were top rated crews taken from other squadrons. Navigators were regarded as the *"Kings"* (e.g. Ken) and pilots who were the *"Wizards"*. These were the men who would find and mark the targets for the bombers, which was even more difficult at night. In bomber squadrons a navigator was of course an essential member of the crew, but in the Pathfinders he was the kingpin. The aircraft had to be over the target precisely on the "dot" (i.e. at the pre-agreed time and location). Although Ken was often the senior officer by rank, the pilot (of whatever rank) was captain of the aircraft.

In 1942, the methods initially employed by Pathfinders were quite basic. The first concept was that each Pathfinder crew should go in first to drop three or four flares to establish the target. Then they would circle around the target for a second time and drop the rest of the flares, once they were sure of the exact position. This method had weak points, because an aircraft could only carry a certain number of flares and if the pilot wasn't sure where he was after the first drop, he did not want to waste any more flares, lest there weren't enough to light up the target for the main bomber force.

In early 1943, Pathfinders developed a much-improved strategy. They were allocated a large "incendiary" bomb and the Pathfinder crews were divided into three categories – "Finders", "Illuminators" and "Markers". "Finders" would go in first and drops rows and rows of flares to light up the whole area of the target. "Illuminators" would then arrive and narrow the target area down. Finally, the "Markers" would go in and drop the large incendiary bombs, which the main force would use as their aiming point.

On 27th July 1943, Ken's father George wrote to him at Wyton congratulating him on the Bar to his DFC (in other words two DFCs). He wrote his letter stating that it was "from a proud and humble father to a brave and noble son". He goes on to say that "There can't be many more in the RAF with a better record than you". George mentions that Ken was due on leave in early August and asked him if he would like Yvonne (his girlfriend) to come to stay at their house in Coventry. George was concerned that she might be upset at seeing the destruction caused by all the bombing. He finished by pleading with Ken not to try and "go for a VC", as he felt that Ken had done enough already. Ken was actually shot down on the same day, 27th July 1943, so the letter never reached him and was returned to his father. Ken read it for the first time in June 1945!

Ken was awarded the Pathfinder Force badge on 2nd August

1943 but was unaware of this award until his release from prisoner of war (POW) camp, although he knew he might be entitled to it. Air Commodore Don Bennett, in charge of the Pathfinder force had written earlier to him on 1st March 1943 saying he had qualified for the badge.

Ken would have been grounded after his 60th trip and with his experience, would more than likely have been allocated to the training needs of future navigators. Navigators were extremely valued! They were responsible for getting the Bombers to their targets and safely returning home - in many cases it had taken two and half years training from joining the RAF for the navigators to be ready for operations. This represented a big investment for the taxpayer, as so many aircrew died within six months of qualifying - the attrition rate was quite appalling. During WW2 75,446 aircrew were killed, wounded or taken prisoner of War (60% of all the aircrew who took part in sorties).

As Station Navigation Officer based at Wyton, he was not supposed to fly regularly, but on the 27th July 1943 a Canadian Navigator, Flying Officer George Hodder, approached him saying he was due to fly to Duisburg, Germany on a reconnaissance trip in a Mosquito that evening. The Hodder said he had met a girl, whom he wanted to take out that evening and asked if Ken could find a replacement navigator. Ken responded by saying that since no-one else was available, he would take his place as part of the two-man crew.

According to Ken's logbook this was the first time he had flown in a Mosquito and he felt quite confident he would return safely. The Mosquito was a fighter bomber built in 1941 of predominately moulded wood. In 1942/43 it was the fastest plane used by any air force, including the Axis powers. It could fly at 378 mph, at a height of 28,000 ft and had a range of 1,905 miles.

However, this was not to be. On their return flight from Germany, they were hit by "flak" from an 88mm German gun located in Holland. The plane quickly caught fire and both the pilot – Flying Officer Edward Snider and Ken were forced to bail out. The Canadian, whom Ken had replaced, was 6ft 2ins and Ken was 5ft 8ins. The parachute was set up for the taller man and so when Ken jumped and pulled the ripcord to open the parachute, the loose straps between his legs caused considerable pain to the extent that the author is lucky to be here!

Snider also survived the bail out and didn't know that Ken was safe until they met again in Stalag Luft 111 in October 1943.

CHAPTER 4

The Lancaster Bomber and the Aircrew experience

AVRO LANCASTER

The Avro Lancaster was a four engine heavy bomber which evolved from the poorly powered twin engine Avro Manchester. A total of 6,924 Lancasters were built between October 1941 and May 1945. Of these 3,249 were shot down in action and 1,005 were destroyed in training or non- combat accidents. During most of WW2 the RAF bombed at night, whereas the US Air Force bombed during the day – their B17 (Flying Fortress) bombers being better armed (having machine gun turrets under the aircraft) than their RAF equivalents (with no machine guns in the belly of the plane), therefore they were better able to ward off Luftwaffe fighters attacking from below. The Lancaster had guns at the front and rear of the aircraft and an upper mid-section gun turret but had an Achilles heel in that it didn't possess any machine gun turrets under the aircraft, which made it extremely vulnerable to attack from beneath. A tactic used by the Luftwaffe was known as "Schräge Musik", which was a common name for the fitting of an upward-firing autocannon or machine gun, to an interceptor aircraft, such as a Messerschmitt 110 night fighter. They flew directly underneath the bomber and fired directly up into the fuselage or engines with deadly efficiency! The first the bomber crew knew was 20mm cannon fire exploding in the bomber or the engines – often too late to take evasive action. The decision not to equip Lancasters with under fuselage guns was taken by Commander in Chief Air Marshall Arthur "Bomber" Harris, who felt it was more important to carry radar equipment rather than extra machine guns. This failure left bombers virtually defenceless during the most intense phase of night bombing of Germany, from June 1943 to July 1944. More Lancasters were shot down from below than from any other quarter. Lack of ventral defensive armament (machine guns located under the planes) cost the lives of many thousands of aircrew who might otherwise have survived had this defensive error been properly realised and addressed.

One of the defensive measures that Lancasters were able to perform was to "corkscrew" (which is where an aircraft could turn and descend rapidly, hence the word "corkscrew"). This was an amazing aerial feat considering that a fully loaded Lancaster weighed 30 tons. It was a very resilient aircraft in terms of its airframe. A good pilot would listen to the gunners who would warn of fighters and tell the pilot when to start the "controlled spin". The gunners would advise whether to dive starboard (right) or port (left), so they would have the best chance of evading whatever fighter was attacking them. Between 1942 and 1945, Lancasters flew 156,000 sorties and dropped 618,378 tons of bombs.

So what was it like for aircrews flying bombers over Germany at night in 1942/43?

Ken did not talk much about his many sorties, facing death night after night in an aircraft packed with high explosives, incendiaries and high octane fuel. We have anecdotal evidence and various jottings about his experiences. The seven man crew were from all walks of life and he did comment on the camaraderie and teamwork of each crew needed for each operation.

An example of a typical trip is to be found on 31st October 1944 on a sortie to Cologne (after Ken had been shot down). Sixteen Lancasters of 153 Squadron with their sixteen navigators, few of them older than twenty-four were sent to bomb Cologne. All sixteen of 153 squadron returned safely to Scampton that night, although two Lancasters were shot down out of the total of 493 bombers on the raid from various squadrons sent out that evening.

Although clear skies would be ideal conditions for a raid, they were also ideal for the German anti-aircraft gunners and night fighters seeking to destroy the intruders. Fully loaded, a Lancaster weighed nearly 30 tons, and one of which took off every two minutes to make up the large bomber formations (as many as 1,000 aircraft in some raids). The navigator teams were briefed by the Navigation Leader (in a separate room away from the rest of the crew) as to the route to and from Cologne, and the return course which would be different from their outward one. The Navigation Leader would have provided times, speeds, heights and the strength of winds they would encounter and also the estimated time of arrival over the target. The navigators would then join up with the rest of the crew to hear the Station Commander give them a brief "pep" talk. Near to the take-off time, the pilots and gunners went out to their aircraft, with navigators following thirty minutes later, after all the physical checks and instrument tests on the aircraft had been run through.

They departed late evening (2200) and arrived back 8 hours later, early in the morning. The Lancasters took off at 100mph and climbed to 16,000 feet. The navigator would track their actual location by radar checks every six minutes. This was vitally important so that they kept the correct distance between themselves and the other bombers in the raid. Flying at 20,000 feet meant outside temperatures could be as low as minus 20 degrees centigrade and although navigators were issued with gloves, they would have found it very difficult wearing them to draw pencil lines, operate a protractor or calculator, so their only choice was to work with freezing hands.

At this time, unlike the Americans, they had no fighter escort once

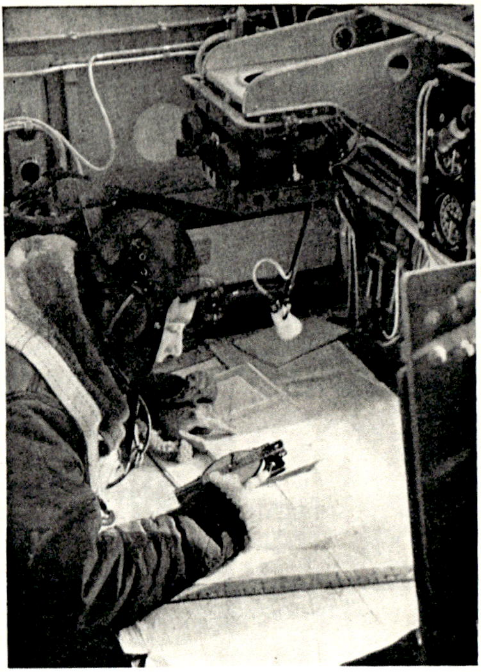

THE NAVIGATOR PLOTS HIS COURSE

At his station in a Stirling bomber the navigator is busy calculating his course. Upon this very important member of the air crew the success of the bombing raid may depend. Besides plotting the aircraft's course the navigator is also responsible for aiming the bombs

THE NAVIGATOR PLOTS HIS COURSE

they got over the Channel. All crews were nervous, but these feelings were put to one side once the aircraft left the ground and the crew went into a busy routine. The navigators were vital to make sure the plane was heading in the right direction and height (so as not to hit other aircraft in the formation). Flying over the Dutch coast they often encountered light flak (small anti-aircraft fire), but at this stage the flak was of no great concern.

It was closer to and indeed over the target that things got really scary (in the widest sense of the word). Heavy flak and shells exploded around the aircraft. Searchlights were seen as a nuisance, as long as your plane wasn't coned (i.e. all German search lights were on you). This attracted flak and fighters jumped in very quickly on seeing a "lit up" bomber. Being in a coned aircraft would have been a very frightening experience for the crew, particularly if they had yet to release their bombs.

If bombers were particularly unlucky they would be "pinned" by a radio controlled searchlight, whose details would then be passed to other searchlights allowing the enemy gunners and fighters to easily find and "cone" the bomber. Of course, the most dangerous time in the flight for bombers was at the approach to the release point, where the Lancaster had to fly absolutely straight and level on the bombing run to the targets already lit up by flares from Pathfinders.

Over their target in Cologne, they released their bomb load at 17,500 feet. The bombers then turned for home, which also had its difficulties as the German night fighters would have been alerted to their presence. Once their bombs had been dropped, the navigator's job was to set a plan for the route home. Quite often this was done with just three or even two out of the four engines working – the other two possibly having been hit by cannon. Another terrifying experience was fire inside an aircraft - the thought of being burned alive was too great to contemplate.

The Lancasters of 153 Squadron all got back safely that trip, but many crews struggled to make it back to their base in England due to damage and had to land at airfields other than their own. On arrival back home they were told who had sadly been lost and they were debriefed as to their own experiences. All crews would have similarly been debriefed and then like most airmen, under the most enormous strain, set off for a few beers to the local pub, living in anticipation of a similar trip the next evening.

We will never fully appreciate how these young men lived under such stress, not knowing if the next trip was going to be the last! They were expected to put losses to the back of their minds and the mental stress was on-going and considerable. Counselling belonged to the future and aircrew had to cope with it as best they could. Ken's family are convinced his colitis, in the late 1950s, was a result of this ongoing stress (as was he).

If you should ever visit the RAF Museum in Hendon, North London, you will see a Lancaster (Q-Queenie – now S-Sugar, R5868) on display. As we see from his logbook, Ken actually flew in this specific Lancaster on 25th July 1943 over Essen in Germany! On this occasion they had a special passenger – General Arnold of the USAAF. Up to that point the USAAF did not believe that the RAF were taking the same risks as the USAAF, who flew during the day. After the flight General Arnold admitted this was incorrect and testified to the courage of the RAF in general based on this mission. It is possible to see and read the painted inscription on the side of Queenie – " No enemy plane will fly over Reich territory" – a boast by Hermann

QUEENIE FROM TRIP – NOTE INSCRIPTION

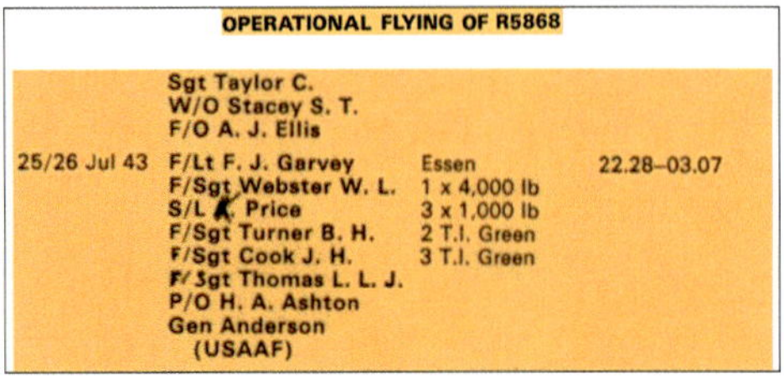

OPERATIONAL FLYING OF R5868

	Sgt Taylor C. W/O Stacey S. T. F/O A. J. Ellis		
25/26 Jul 43	F/Lt F. J. Garvey F/Sgt Webster W. L. S/L K. Price F/Sgt Turner B. H. F/Sgt Cook J. H. F/Sgt Thomas L. L. J. P/O H. A. Ashton Gen Anderson (USAAF)	Essen 1 x 4,000 lb 3 x 1,000 lb 2 T.I. Green 3 T.I. Green	22.28–03.07

QUEENIE LOG BOOK & KGP LOG BOOK
JULY 1943

Goering, a high Nazi party member who was in charge of the German Luftwaffe.

A poignant moment for Ken and his family occurred just a month before he passed away in April 1980, when the family obtained special permission from the Museum to visit this particular aircraft and to once again sit in the very same navigator's seat which he had occupied on July 25th 1943, but in a much safer setting! It was a very moving moment for both Ken and his close family and we are extremely grateful to the RAF Museum for making this possible.

Ken Nav seat April 1980 & KGP & Sqd Leader Diamond March 1980

Queenie's last operational flight (part of 125 bombers) was a trip to bomb Berchtesgaden – Hitler's mountain retreat, which she helped duly flatten!

KEN IN LANCASTER NAVIGATOR SEAT
MARCH 1980

KEN & SQD LEADER DIAMOND
MARCH 1980

CHAPTER 5

Bombing - The Moral Dilemma!

In the 1960s the author recalls a conversation between his father and an older man called Charles Fisher in a pub in Iver about the issues of killing people in war. Charles had been a machine gunner on the Somme in WW1 and whilst he knew he had killed many German soldiers, who obviously were in uniform, his view was that it was either them or us, so he felt he had no choice. He asked my father about how he felt about the mass bombing of German cities (e.g. Dresden) and the resultant enormous loss of life amongst the civilian population. Ken declined to comment other than to say carpet bombing ("carpet bombing" is the total destruction of a town or area by saturation bombing) is what they had been instructed to undertake by Air Chief Marshall Sir Arthur Harris, Air Officer Commanding-in-Chief Bomber Command, commonly known as Bomber Harris. Although Ken never actually expressed his view, the author strongly believes that he would have been unhappy at this mass killing of civilians and yet there was nothing he could do about it.

Bomber Harris said in May 1942 in support of mass bombing of German towns that *"Germany faces an air attack which will make the bombing of Britain in the winter of 1940/41 insignificant. He went on to say that we will bomb Germany so persistently and so severely her power to make war will be crippled."* The largest weight of bombs dropped by the Germans was less than 450 tons on London (population at the time 4.4 million) on 10th May 1941. On 9th August 1942 the RAF dropped 450 tons on Osnabruck (population 89,000) and this was repeated all over Germany. The question still remains to this day, as to whether blanket bombing of Germany brought a swifter end to WW2.

In March 1942, Harris was appointed by Sir Winston Churchill to carry out indiscriminate area bombing in an effort to smash the German home front into collapse. In November 1944, Harris claimed that Bomber Command had destroyed 45 out of 60 leading German cities, but still it didn't reduce Germany's ability to produce tanks and planes in great numbers. The bombing of Hamburg and Dresden and the resultant fire storms and civilian casualties caused questions to be asked of their legitimacy, notably after the war. The bombing campaign was indeed terrible, but in the context of the time, essential. In May 1943, Richard Stokes, MP for Ipswich, stated in the House of Commons, that there was a growing volume of opinion in the UK that indiscriminate bombing of civilians was both morally wrong and strategic lunacy. In his victory broadcast on 13th May 1945 Churchill omitted any tribute to Bomber Command or the role that it had played in winning the war and no campaign medal was struck for those who took part. This was corrected only in very recent years, when Ken (long after he died) received a clasp signifying his role in the RAF. Even in the post war period, there was animosity towards those who flew in Bomber Command. Eventually the Bomber Command Memorial was opened in June 2012 at Green Park, London to commemorate all 55,573 bomber aircrew who had died in WW2.

In September 1961, Sefton Delmer, a journalist interviewed a number of key German figures as to the effectiveness of blanket bombing. Ariel bombing was intended by Harris to undermine the Germans will to resist, but Hans Brunswig, Hamburg's Deputy Fire chief at the time insisted that it did not. The German people were alerted to the raids and were able to get to the shelters. Shipbuilder Willy Schlieker told Delmer that had the RAF adopted a more strategic bombing plan to attack oil installations and rail marshalling yards, it would have caused the Germans many more problems in continuing the war. As it was, blanket bombing encouraged the Germans to produce armaments, in much smaller factory units, in areas away from large conurbations.

Like many ex-servicemen of his generation, as a child, I don't recall my father talking much about his time during the war, and got the feeling it was something he didn't wish to remember. I do know he was very reluctant to holiday in Europe until the mid 1960's.

BOMBER COMMAND MEMORIAL AT GREEN PARK, LONDON

CHAPTER 6

Ken's missing!

DE HAVILAND MOSQUITO

Picking up Ken's story from chapter three we find him flying in a Mosquito (a two man, twin engine light bomber / reconnaissance aircraft) on July 27th 1943. Ken felt sure of his return as he would have been aware that the aircraft was the fastest and highest flying at the time. Chance flak, however, caught them and he and the pilot had to bail out.

The following day, 28th July 1943, RAF Wyton sent a telegram to Ken's parents in Coventry saying the following:

"Very much regret to inform you that your son Squadron Leader Kenneth George Price failed to return from operations on the night of 27/28th July 1943. Letter follows. Any further information received will be immediately communicated to you. RAF Wyton."

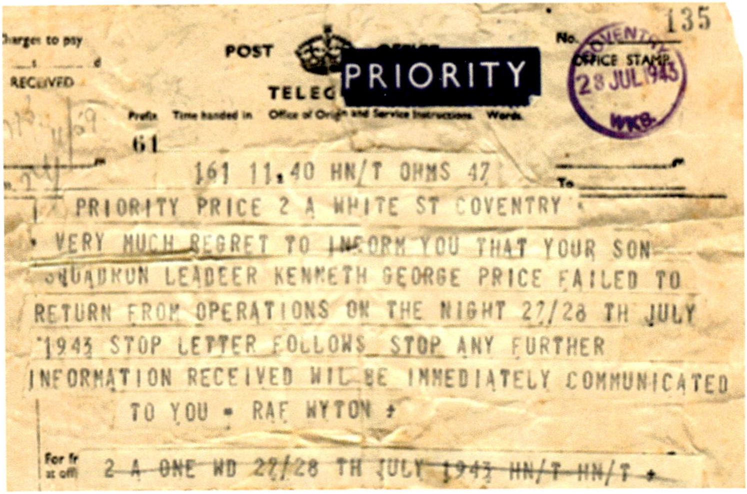

harges to pay
RECEIVED
POST
TELEG
PRIORITY
No. 135
COVENTRY OFFICE STAMP 28 JUL 1943 WKB
Prefix Time handed in Office of Origin and Service Instructions Words
61
161 11.40 HN/T OHMS 47
To
PRIORITY PRICE 2 A WHITE ST COVENTRY
VERY MUCH REGRET TO INFORM YOU THAT YOUR SON SQUADRON LEADEER KENNETH GEORGE PRICE FAILED TO RETURN FROM OPERATIONS ON THE NIGHT 27/28 TH JULY 1943 STOP LETTER FOLLOWS STOP ANY FURTHER INFORMATION RECEIVED WIL BE IMMEDIATELY COMMUNICATED TO YOU = RAF WYTON +
2 A ONE WD 27/28 TH JULY 1943 HN/T HN/T +

COPY OF TELEGRAM FROM RAF WYTON

On the same day George Price, Ken's father, also received a letter from Group Captain H Graham, Station Commander at Wyton to say Ken was missing. He also took the occasion to compliment Ken on his high standard of navigation and that it was this that had contributed much to the success of the squadron. He went on to say his personal effects were being taken care of and they would be in touch again shortly.

An article in the Coventry Evening Telegraph on 29th July 1943 appeared under the heading "Coventry Air Officer missing" – this commented that Ken had been a member of their commercial staff since 1937, had joined the RAF Reserve in 1938, been awarded the DFC and that he was also a keen table tennis player. They were obviously very proud of Ken's service to his country!

On 5th August 1943 Ken's father George wrote to the British Red Cross in London to enquire if they knew if he had been taken as a POW. He wasn't to hear anymore until 3rd September 1943, that he had in fact become a POW.

On 6th August 1943, Ken's father received a letter from the RAF Benevolent Fund offering financial support if required, if Ken was the main provider to the household. Ken's father did not take up the offer.

It was in late August 1943, before it was known that Ken was safe as a POW, that Douglas, Ken's identical twin brother flew to Wyton from Iceland, (where he was based). Apparently Douglas had gone to his Commanding Officer at the Coastal Command unit in Iceland and said that by telepathy he knew his twin brother was missing, but had survived and that he wished to leave in order to back to England to comfort his parents. His Commanding Officer apparently had the good sense to believe him and grant him the leave which he requested, as well as the means of transport to England. On arrival in England he went to his parents to assure them that his twin brother was alive and well. He then went to Pathfinder Headquarters and presented himself to Group Captain H Graham, the Station Commander at the camp. Group Captain Graham was "allegedly stunned", as he apparently said to Douglas "What are you doing here Ken, I thought you had been shot down over Europe". Douglas then had to explain that he was not Ken, but an identical twin who wanted to re-assure the Group Captain that he had a strong fraternal feeling (that only close twins seem to possess) that Ken was safe – which thankfully turned out to be the case, following a communication received from the Red Cross on 3rd September 1943. This was a truly wonderful example of the power of telepathy at times of great human stress.

Ken had landed in Holland, twisting his ankle in the process and injuring his face on the side of the burning machine, as he had been unable to get a clear jump. He landed in a hayfield under blistering sun, with Germans tending the field and within talking range. He was parched with thirst and unable to move, but was not discovered. Lunch time intervened with the Germans leaving, so he quickly disposed of his parachute and managed to walk into a nearby village, where a Dutch boy gave him water. He was then picked up by the Dutch Resistance who persuaded him to get rid of his "dog tags" – in retrospect wrongly. Dog tags were worn around the neck by most military personnel to help identify casualties. It was metal and had the wearer's name & blood group, as well as religious preferences. There were two tags, so that one would be returned to the "authorities" advising of his death and the other kept with the body for identification. The Dutch Resistance also exchanged his uniform for peasant's clothes and he spent 8 days walking through Holland.

After the war, Ken told a neighbour in Iver, David Oldcorn, that he walked westwards (following the sun and silk map) after baling out and David asked him if he ever came across German soldiers. Ken's answer was "yes" and he then "ran like hell". He said he could easily outrun them, as the Germans were loaded with heavy coats, backpacks and rifles – David feels that there may have been a degree of exaggeration here, which Ken was prone to, on occasions.

The resistance then placed him in a Catholic Church, which they viewed as a safe refuge, but Ken was betrayed to the Gestapo (German secret police) by the Catholic priest, who was scared he would be shot for harbouring a British flyer "on the run".

The Gestapo accused Ken of being a spy, partly because he could speak German quite well, but more importantly he had no dog tags to identify himself and he was in civilian clothing. He was kept in solitary confinement for 2 weeks. The Gestapo beat him and certainly broke some of his ribs in the process. It was alleged that he was to be taken out to be shot, but this was never corroborated. Ken survived by being "rescued" by a Luftwaffe officer (German air force), who said he believed his story. This "officer" subsequently turned out to be Sergeant Takob Wachowiak of the SS (under Heinrich Himmler). We have no evidence but suspect this intervention was meant to put Ken at ease, in order to release more information on his background. You will hear more of Wachowiak later in the book. POWs under the Geneva Convention (of which Germany was a signatory) were required to give just their name, rank and number on capture. It is interesting that most POWs were given a form by the Germans, purporting to be issued by the Red Cross, which did in fact ask for details of the operation and home base. The interrogating officer informed the POW that if the form was completed, it would be immediately transmitted to Geneva and their next of kin would know that he was fit and well. It was known by this time however, that these so called Red Cross forms were a product of German Intelligence, so most POWs (including Ken) declined to complete them and simply declared what was required under the Geneva Convention.

Most airmen (including Ken) had received some basic training by MI9 in what to expect on being shot down, captured and interrogated by the Germans and a little of their methods. They highlighted that under the Geneva Convention of 1929, prisoners were only required to give their name, rank and number. MI9 highlighted that very often microphones were hidden in huts to hear unguarded remarks by prisoners. They also advised aircrew that the Germans used "phoney medical officers" who were in reality interrogators; and also used "stool pigeons" to infiltrate aircrew - these were enemy personnel, disguised as fellow prisoners of war.

It is worth commenting that British prisoners had a major advantage over POWs of other European countries, in that Britain was not under occupation. This meant the Germans could not take out reprisals against their families and friends, if British POWs attempted to escape. In Nazi occupied Europe, those caught aiding Allied airmen endangered not only their own lives, but also their entire family. This situation changed dramatically after the Great Escape from Stalag Luft 111, as you will read later.

The Gestapo are alleged to have said to Ken that they would have no hesitation in shooting him, as he was part of the "terror flyers" who were bombing the Ruhr. They neglected the fact that the Luftwaffe had previously bombed Warsaw, Rotterdam, Belgrade, London and Coventry without any regard for their inhabitants, prior to this activity by the RAF. This was a consistent response by the Germans to the bombing of their own country, which seems quite strange considering their actions in bombing other countries with impunity and that they had initiated the practice.

CHAPTER 7

Transfer to POW Camp

Ken was taken to Dulag Luft (an abbreviation from Durchgangslager der Luftwaffe – being a transit camp for air force crew who had been shot down) in Germany on 21st August 1943. This was a camp for all air force prisoners and wasn't dependent on rank. It was located at Oberursel, at the foot of the Taunus mountains. On arrival at the gates of Dulag Luft, the prisoners were channelled in several directions depending on the physical layout of the camp at various junctures during the war. Initially the camp was under the jurisdiction of the German Army, but as the number of downed airmen grew it was transferred to the Luftwaffe in December 1939. When the number of captured airmen continued to increase in 1940, the authorities were forced to add a 65 bed hospital for injured prisoners. Ken spent 2 weeks in this hospital in August 1943, recovering from his time with the Gestapo.

As early as 1940, prisoners had developed a method of using coded messages to send and receive messages to and from London. Messages from prisoners were within letters sent home and information for the existing POWs was gleaned from newly arrived aircrew, who had been only recently been shot down.

The first communication that Ken had with his parents in Coventry was via a postcard dated 21st August 1943 from Dulag Luft in Germany, which arrived in England on 27th September 1943.

Ken said:

"Dear All, You will doubtless be surprised at my new address. I had to part company with my aircraft when the machine caught fire, but I landed safely. Please look after my uniform & a cinema projector I bought recently, it is valuable. I am quite fit & well & taking a long needed rest. I'll write you a letter in a few days. My address is Dulag Luft Germany. Please write to me love Ken."

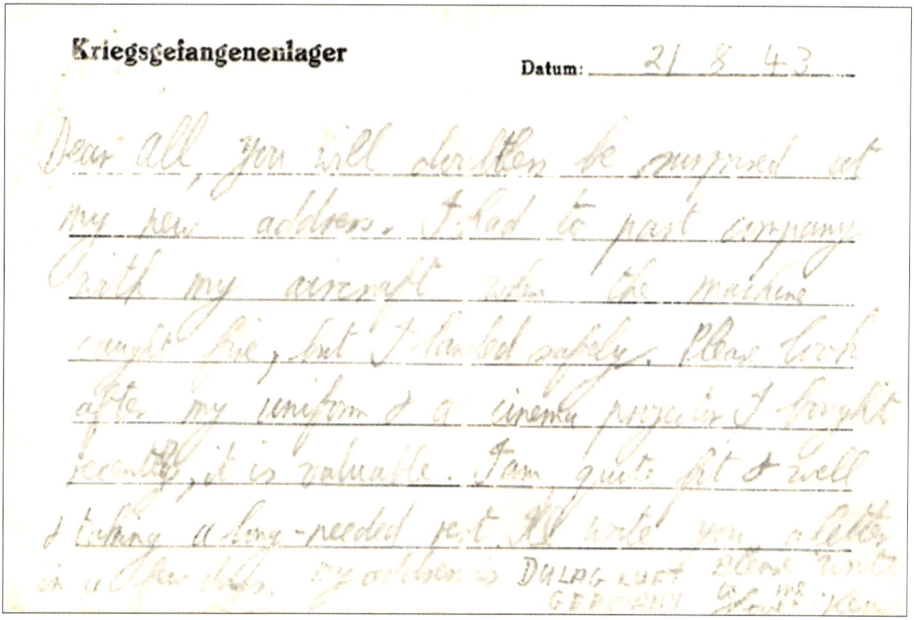
Kriegsgefangenenlager Datum: 21 8 43

Dear all, you will doubtless be surprised at my new address. I had to part company with my aircraft when the machine caught fire, but I landed safely. Please look after my uniform & a cinema projector I bought recently, it is valuable. I am quite fit & well & taking a long-needed rest. I'll write you a letter in a few days. My address is DULAG LUFT GERMANY. Please write love Ken

One of the first escapes from Dulag Luft was in June 1941 by 18 prisoners. All were recaptured, but security was tightened after this event, although the Camp remained under the control of the Luftwaffe. The Germans attempts to keep close tabs on prisoners was frustrated by the "duty pilot" scheme. The duty pilot was a POW who sat at a window offering a good view of the front gate and he kept a record of all German movements, so could alert, in good time, those involved in any kinds of forbidden work (e.g. tunnelling).

Ken was transferred to Stalag Luft 111, Sagan on the Polish

border on 26th August 1943, about 60 miles from the German Border and 100 miles South East of Berlin. It was a camp for RAF officers, but the name Stalag was misleading, as it was a contraction of the German word Stamnlager, meaning a prison for "common stock". In reality few non- commissioned officers (NCOs) and other lower rank prisoners were sent to Luft 111 – the POWs being mainly comprising "officers".

Ken sent a letter to his parents on 27th August 1943, which arrived in Coventry on 16th October 1943. Ken talks about having been moved to Stalag Luft 111, which will be his permanent Camp from now on. He says his POW number is 2193 and in it he comments on the Red Cross parcels without which they would surely have died due to the poor supply of food from the Germans. He specifically asks to be sent glove , a roll neck sweater and blanket, as he says it gets very cold in that part of Poland in the winter. Ken sent further letters on 28th August and 3rd September, where the German censor seems to have had a "field day" with his black ink. In both letters, Ken talks about the lack of food utensils, which had to be made out of empty food cans, he also asks for chocolate & cigarettes to be sent, to enable him to barter with the guards.

Luft 111 was only about half a mile from Sagan itself, a town of about 25,000 people with no special claim to fame, apart from a fairly important railway junction, from which prisoners could hear the clanking of ladened goods trains trundling to and from the Russian Front. Sagan was in Silesia and had dry dusty soil, which was easy to dig for the inevitable tunnelling operations, but was also dangerously crumbly. Another point of interest was that it was the furthest point of advance of the Russian forces in WW1. This point was marked by a small cross on a pedestal just outside north compound.

Another Stalag Luft 111 inmate, Flight Lieutenant Jack Lyons, was shot down in a Whitley bomber (slow twin engine aircraft) over Germany in 1941. He says he was picked up by a German soldier and taken to a local Luftwaffe base, where he had lunch and drinks in the local Officers' Mess. He goes on to say that, at every stage, he was courteously treated with no distinction of rank and there was no attempt to obtain information. He was then escorted to Dulag Luft transit camp by a senior NCO and two privates.

THE AUTHOR WITH JACK LYONS IN OCTOBER 2017

Lyons commented that whilst in Dulag Luft, there were four men in a room, with access to hot showers in the barracks. Apparently Red Cross parcels were so plentiful that 4/5 course dinners had to be given at least twice a month, added to which the Germans gave them supplies of wines and spirits that they had liberated during their invasion of France. This situation lasted in some guise until 1942, when the Germans were experiencing setbacks notably in North Africa. It was then that prisoners, who were deemed as possibly having useful information, were sent immediately into solitary confinement.

How different was Ken's experience when he was shot down only two years later, by which time aircrew were known as "killers" by the German populace (encouraged by Joseph Goebbels, Reich Minister of Propaganda from 1933 to 1945). Until the end of 1943, there had been only isolated cases of shot down aircrew being severely abused or killed by civilians. However, after the Allies commenced mass bombing raids on major conurbations (eg Cologne/Dresden) personal attacks posed a major risk to aircrew, if they were shot down. In May 1944, Joseph Goebbels stated that Anglo-American air attacks over Germany were no longer warfare, but "murder pure and simple" (he referred to Allied flyers as Luftgangsters). It was known that in that year a number of Allied flyers had been lynched by civilians, with the German police taking no action to stop them. These officials knew that this lack of action was in gross violation of the Geneva Convention.

In 1942 on transfer to Stalag Luft 111, most POWs did not leave Dulag Luft with any sense of guilt, sincerely believing that they had not given any important information to the Germans. They did however leave with a heightened respect for German thoroughness, organisation and intelligence-gathering ability. On arrival from Dulag Luft to Stalag Luft 111 the "kriegies" (prisoners) were purged, which meant they were fully debriefed by the Senior British Officer as to their movements, since they were shot down and also any update on the progress of the war.

On 3rd September 1943, The Air Ministry in London sent a telegram to Ken's parents in Coventry saying the following:

"Information received through the International Red Cross Committee states that your son A/S /LDR Kenneth George Price DFC is a prisoner of war in German hands. Letter confirming this to follow."

On 4th September 1943 the Coventry Evening Telegraph reported that they had heard that Squadron Leader Kenneth Price, reported missing at the end of July, was now a prisoner of war in Germany.

In the Coventry Telegraph Welfare Record of December 1943, they said that in September they had learnt that Ken was a prisoner of war in Germany, which made comforting reading after the fears that they had harboured for his safety. They went on to say that it had brought forth a shoal of congratulations from his colleagues in the forces, which the Record passes on to him along with the good wishes of those at home. It was an irony of fate that he should reply to messages of congratulation on receiving the DFC from his new

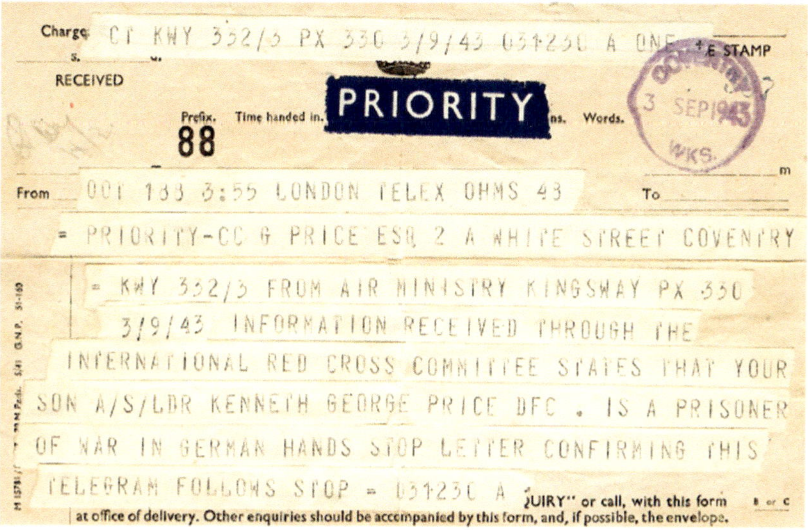

Charge CT KWY 332/3 PX 330 3/9/43 031230 A ONE ... E STAMP

RECEIVED

PRIORITY

Prefix. 88 Time handed in. ... ns. Words.

3 SEP 1943 WKS.

From OCT 133 3:55 LONDON TELEX OHMS 43 To

= PRIORITY-CC G PRICE ESQ 2 A WHITE STREET COVENTRY

= KWY 332/3 FROM AIR MINISTRY KINGSWAY PX 330 3/9/43 INFORMATION RECEIVED THROUGH THE INTERNATIONAL RED CROSS COMMITTEE STATES THAT YOUR SON A/S/LDR KENNETH GEORGE PRICE DFC . IS A PRISONER OF WAR IN GERMAN HANDS STOP LETTER CONFIRMING THIS TELEGRAM FOLLOWS STOP = 031230 A

...UIRY" or call, with this form at office of delivery. Other enquiries should be accompanied by this form, and, if possible, the envelope.

address: "M Stammlager Luft 111". Among the many letters he received was one from Lord Iliffe, Chairman of the Coventry Evening Telegraph to whom Ken replied, thanking his Lordship for the letter and congratulations.

Ken's parents were issued with a fifteen page handbook entitled "For the information of relatives and friends of prisoners of war". It covered many questions that would have been posed by relatives and attempted to answer them. The conditions of prisoners were covered by the Geneva Convention in 1929 to which both the German and Italian Governments were signatories, although initially both were in breach regarding the provision of food and clothing. Switzerland was the protecting power and it was their role to make sure that the Convention principles were being followed. With their greater involvement, Red Cross parcels were getting through to the POWs who desperately needed them. It highlighted that officers (including Ken) should receive pay from the Germans to the equivalent of an officer of corresponding rank in the German forces.

It was interesting to note that only a few days earlier, after it was known he was a prisoner of war, RAF Wyton sent an itemised list of all Ken's personal effects to his father on 21st September 1943, which included items as small as a comb, table tennis bat and 2 coloured pencils.

CHAPTER 8

Life in Stalag Luft 111, Poland

POWs were allowed to send cards back to the UK every week and at this time the German censors didn't initially use their black ink to cover any incriminating information (or what they deemed as incriminating). Later in the war this changed, as can be seen from subsequent cards and letters home. The post from the camps was sent via the International Red Cross in Geneva, Switzerland.

HUTS. STALAG – LUFT -111

Stalag Luft 111, Sagan was built by Polish POWs in 1942 and had huts which were made of wood, and on stilts to enable the German guards to see if any tunnelling was taking place. The Germans assigned to anti-escape duties were called "ferrets." They were German security guards, usually in blue overalls, who patrolled compounds constantly to counter any escape activity, (at least, that was the plan!) The huts were also built on sand, which made tunnelling exceedingly difficult, both in their maintenance and in terms of disposing of the sand, which was a different colour from the surface earth of the camp. Ferrets were watched by stooges, who were the POWs own "sentries", to warn escape workers whenever ferrets approached.

German guards were nicknamed "goons", and when asked by Germans what it meant, they were told in meant "German officer or non-com". Allegedly, the Germans never did understand that it was the way of POWs showing their negative feelings towards their captors.

POWs adopted a practice of "goon baiting" whenever possible, which was to do whatever they could to upset the Germans routine and general sense of composure. The forms of activity ranged from the humorous to barbaric.

On the humorous side, there was a young German work camp located just outside Luft 111 and they went off to work each morning with their shovels over their shoulders, they would be singing German marching songs. 200 prisoners stood by the fence singing "Hi Ho, Hi Ho, it's off to work we go" from Snow White and the Seven Dwarfs. The Germans were not amused and after a short while avoided walking past the camp. One of the more serious forms of goon baiting was harassing the ferrets, as they probed under the huts looking for tunnels. There is a case where prisoners were "allegedly" cleaning their huts with boiling water and letting the water run through the floorboards, when a German ferret was underneath.

In 1944, it was estimated that there were around 240 POW camps in Germany and Poland holding about 9 million men and at some point in 1944 Sagan housed 10,000 POWs in five compounds – north compound where Ken was located housed 1,500 RAF officers! Contrary to the 1963 film The Great Escape, there were actually no Americans in north compound. The south compound built in the latter part of 1942 and early 1943 housed the increasing number of Americans who had been shot down. The whole camp had 500 to 600 German guards, mainly Luftwaffe, who were too old to fight – being over 50 years old.

Ground microphones were installed shortly after the north compound was built, at depths of three yards below the ground, and at intervals of 32 yards along the perimeter fence. These contained a highly sensitive swinging pen which was set in motion by the slightest disturbance in the ground. The noise was registered through a microphone and transmitted by cable to the central listening post in the Kommandanteur (the German quarters in the camp).

The first successful escape from Stalag Luft 111 by tunnel was achieved in October 1943, when three prisoners from the east compound used a vaulting horse – the famous "Wooden Horse" – to disguise tunnelling activities. The horse was placed in the same position each day with a constant stream of gymnasts (POWs) vaulting it each day. Having been transferred initially to east camp, Ken became involved in helping this escape by being one of the POWs drafted in to jump over the vaulting horse, whilst the tunnellers worked below. The three men broke out of the tunnel and made their way back to the UK, via Sweden. This escape was immortalised in the film of the same name, which was made in 1950 starring Leo Genn, David Tomlinson and Anthony Steel and was one of the famous war films of its time. Before the escape took place, Ken was moved to north compound in another part of Stalag Luft 111!

The monotony of camp life made food one of the constantly discussed topics! Speaking of which – the same word covers it all – monotonous! Most of the time each prisoner had one Red Cross parcel per head per week, which provided half the energy value required, the other half came from Reich rations. The total calorie input was around 3,000 per day, when both rations were supplied (which is about the same for a male in 2021). The lack of food was serious in the early days, before the Red Cross had fully got a distribution system set up and in the last six months of the war, when Reich transport had broken down,the German rations fall away. It was subsequently learnt that in 1941 the Germans were stealing part of the Red Cross rations as well. The psychological aspect of food is most interesting for prisoners, as it had a compelling effect on morale.

The POWs had these two primary sources of food – German rations and Red Cross parcels. The German rations were supposed to be the same as for a foreign labour force, in which as RAF officers, they were not required to participate. After the war, the United Nations said that the German ration calorie intake was insufficient to maintain life, so without Red Cross parcels, POWs would have starved – as can be seen from the concentration camp inmates after liberation – those who survived, emerged as little more than skeletons!

AUSCHWITZ CONCENTRATION CAMP SURVIVORS APRIL 1945

German rations comprised per person per day – 1/5th loaf of bread, ingredients (normally rye), 50 grams of sausage of dubious pedigree, variable amounts of margarine and jam and ½ kilo of poor-quality potatoes. The camp cookhouse was also supplied with poor quality meat and vegetables – mainly cabbage.

The Red Cross parcels came from two main sources – Canada and the UK. The quality of those from Canada was superior to the UK, but this was not surprising due to the need to feed the British population and the dreadful effects of the German U boat campaign in the Atlantic, fewer parcels from Canada reached the POW camps.

Red Cross parcels contained a wide range of food items and until later stages of the war, it was one parcel per man per week. Each room held between 6 and 8 men and they (in theory) took it in turns to cook and wash up.

POWS AND A GERMAN GUARD WITH FOOD PARCELS IN THE CAMP IN 1943.

ARTEFACTS THAT CAN BE SEEN AT THE CAMP IN 2019 BOTTOM RIGHT - REPLICA HUT 104

The British Red Cross section of the Prisoner of War Department issued an edict to all in the UK in February 1942 about the supply of food parcels. The aim was to supply each POW with a weekly parcel weighing 11lbs. Originally parcels were addressed to individuals, but in early 1940 this was changed, as prisoners were moved between camps. This meant the parcels were sent in the correct numbers and distributed to all prisoners including new arrivals, so that all got an equal share. The Red Cross parcels packed in Britain were despatched to Lisbon in Portugal (which was a neutral country), then by sea to Marseilles, France and then sent by train to Geneva, Switzerland. This process took between 6 and 8 weeks and got longer as the war progressed.

Next of kin were allowed to send parcels to individuals every 3 months – these items sent included toothpaste, slabs of chocolate and clothing, but would take at least two and more likely three months to reach the recipient.

Towards the end of 1944, food parcels began to dry up due to the state of the war at the time – the Germans were in full retreat across all fronts – and transport from Geneva became very difficult. Men began to lose weight and they were facing the coldest winter on record. It was interesting to note that the German guards didn't fare much better in terms of food rations, which again were in short supply due to the change in war conditions.

XMAS DINNER MENU 1943

Ken kept a menu card from his Christmas 1943 dinner. This said Room 10 Block 112 – Starter Soup – Cream of Bouillon with croutons. Meat – Roast Turkey with white leek sauce, baked potatoes, and mashed carrots. Sweet – Xmas pudding with cream. Coffee – ersatz (made from acorns) almost undrinkable – but the only alternative due to lack of the real thing.

Alcohol in Camp was a rarity, when Germany had exhausted the supplies they had looted from France and began to feel the pinch, so prisoners were well at the bottom of the list for any such luxuries. At Christmas, the Germans distributed to each prisoner about two litres of a horrible travesty of beer. It resembled the genuine article in colour only, but no taste or alcohol, though it was a good exercise for the kidneys. Kriegy ingenuity overcame the liquor problem, in the short term, with a fiery concoction called raisin brew, made from raisins and sugar saved from Red Cross food parcels. It took three weeks to ferment and the residue possessed considerable alcoholic ferocity. The hangovers were frightful, but the first few hours of riotous oblivion were a refreshing anodyne to the atrophying stagnation of prison life. The Senior British Officer banned raisin brew after a big party had got out of hand and the German guards had to regain control by firing over the POWs heads. Unfortunately a young squadron leader was shot in the stomach, hence the banning of the brew.

The north compound, in Stalag Luft 111, received on average about 2,000 Red Cross parcels per week. The contents varied from week to week, according to whether they were from England, Scotland, Canada, and latterly New Zealand or USA. There were often 50 different types of food in these parcels, so if a prisoner didn't like something, for example, fish and would have preferred cheese instead, it was necessary to have some form of exchange, hence the exchange centre which became known as the *"Barbed wire department store called Foodacco!"* The Germans didn't allow any currency at all in the camp, so a system of valuation had to be formed. It was based on a system of points, so, for example corned beef was 65 points, half pound sugar was 80 points, and 2 oz tea was 30 points. Each individual in the camp kept his own account. Foodacco was divided into four sections:

- Food Items
- Tobacco
- Miscellaneous – anything that didn't fall into the other two categories – e.g. clothing, toiletries and music items

- The transfer department, which dealt with the transfer of points from one account to another. An example of how the system worked – a prisoner had a surplus of biscuits and wanted chocolate in exchange. He took his biscuits to the counter and they credited him with 55 points and debited him with 40 points for the chocolate, leaving him with a credit of 15 points.

A small crisis occurred when the compound went on half rations. A panic wave went through the camp with everyone rushing to the shop to redeem their points. A rationing system had to be introduced to give a fair share to everyone, but a black market appeared (as at home) which was difficult to control. Foodacco also acted as a sponsor, so for example 100 and 50 points respectively were given to the winner and loser of every boxing tournament. On 24th December 1944, Foodacco organised a Christmas Fair which included a large number of games and attractions such as roulette, guessing competitions and lucky dip. They guessed that 1944 would be likely to be the last Christmas in the "goon bag", so they threw all their resources at it. In the event, they were correct, as POWs started to march out of the camp at the end of January 1945.

It is worth commenting on food in the camp from both Ken's remarks and those of Ft Lt Jack Lyons, whom the author interviewed in October 2017. The Germans normal interference with Red Cross parcels was to pierce the tins. This was designed to prevent storage for escape purposes. When a security alert was on – e.g .some alleged misbehaviour – all packaging had to be removed including tins, leaving the POWs with the contents only. In the winter this was a bad enough inconvenience, but in the summer it really did present problems. Trying to store meat, fish, sugar, tea, milk powder and biscuits in temperatures often 30 degrees centigrade with no fridge, no larder and no containers was well-nigh impossible – they were forced to use mugs, plates and any saucepans to cook, as well as eat from.

Ken had written under a cartoon reproduced in the Sagan Souvenir book of a cat having been chopped up for food *"Alas for the Commandant's Cat!"*

CARTOON FROM " SPOTLIGHT ON STALAG LUFT 111"

To keep themselves occupied and also to keep fit, many sports were pursued by the inhabitants of the camps, who had little to do during captivity. After the war, The Spotlight on Stalag Luft 111 by Scandriff (the camp newspaper) says that the ever- changing face of the Sagan sports field leaves many vivid and pleasant memories. Soccer proved to be the top favourite in the winter games, due no doubt to the large number of British personnel, although in 1944 ice-hockey was fast becoming a favourite due in part to the influx of American and Canadian prisoners. The very cold winter of 1944/45 allowed for the building of three ice rinks and laying of water to a remarkably high standard. Cricket was very popular in the summer months, as was rugby, although games were limited due to ground conditions and "the shortage of willing victims".

Nearly every POW Camp in Germany had a radio and they all tuned in to hear what the BBC had to say each day on the progress of the war. Radios were strictly banned by the Germans and if they suspected one existed they would search industriously for many months normally with no success, as the radios, after use, were split up into small components, that were easy to hide. These radios were not so difficult to come by, as it was never very hard to find a German who was either dissatisfied, disloyal or greedy, and who with a little gentle bribery could be encouraged to bring radio parts and other useful things into the camp. Ken took part in these activities due to his fluency in German. The Germans were very keen to get hold of cigarettes and chocolate from the POWs. Most of the guards at Sagan were Luftwaffe men, many of whom were WW1 veterans, who wanted only to get back to their families. Much of this undermining was done by inviting the guards in question into a room for a cup of coffee and biscuit. POWs had real coffee from Red Cross parcels and as the Germans hadn't seen real coffee for years, it was rare for the guard to turn down such an invitation. The German speaking POW would sympathise with the guard having to fight Hitler's war and encourage him to air his views on the war in general. After a few weeks the conversation was steered casually to suggest that the POW needed some ink and pen for his artwork. Generally by now the guard obliged in return for chocolate and cigarettes. With a number of contacts carrying out this activity, several guards helped build up contraband of many "verboten" articles that the "X" (the Escape Committee within the camp) needed. Apart from pen and ink (for producing passports and identity cards), they brought in magnets (for compasses), radio parts, cameras, photographic equipment, hammers, saws, pincers and maps of the local countryside. This whole exercise made a valuable contribution to the ongoing escape plans. The forgery department was codenamed "Dean & Dawsons". They used linoleum and rubber to make stamps for forging passes, as well as identity papers, gate passes, railway tickets, German pay books and headed note paper. They also made replica rifles, which were carved from wood, stained with brown polish and metal parts created by filling in with lead from pencils.

CHAPTER 9

Ken's life in Camp

On 12th December 1943, Ken wrote to his father saying how much he adored Yvonne and how he much appreciated his father writing to her. Ken went on to say he hoped that his dad wouldn't have to write to all his girlfriends, as he would have got writer's cramp doing so. Ken also made reference to the Cottage in Earslden, Coventry, which was obviously a favourite "watering hole".

He perfected his German and engaged with guards to gain information and useful items. Once a German guard was hooked, he could be blackmailed into providing further contraband required by potential escapers. In his post war papers, Ken comments that he managed to get a German guard (in return for a piece of chocolate) to give up his pass, which was copied. On another occasion he says that a German guard was encouraged to take off his belt on a hot day. The buckle was then pressed into a mould made out of congealed soup.

Ken commented in post war notes that POWs would steal anything. There was an instance when a German staff car came into the camp and the German speaking POWs flattered the chauffeur, at which point other POWs stole tools and German military books from the car. The books were of course returned to the Germans, but only after copies had been made. He also reports that a dog wandered into the Camp (not the German Shepherd guard dogs) and it was killed and eaten, as they were so hungry. He goes on to say that compasses were made from old, melted gramophone records, magnetised needles and pieces of glass from broken windows. After the war Ken never used a map when driving, he would always simply rely on a compass in the car.

Drawing on his journalistic and editorial experience, Ken was also one of the editors of the camp newspaper called – Scangriff. The name Scangriff was derived from *"Scandal"* press and *"Angriff"*, which was a German newspaper title. This was published weekly and reported on activities in the camp, including meetings between the Senior British Officer and the German Camp Commandant. It also covered mail, coal shortages, availability of educational books, ice hockey matches and the ongoing need to repair broken hockey sticks. The first issue of this newspaper was in March 1944.

Ken was also involved in the camp theatre, which the Germans actively supported as they felt it would keep the POWs occupied and "out of mischief". They even provided materials for the shows! Ken helped produce shows and acted in them as well. It was here he met Roy Dotrice, Peter Butterworth, Bernard Cribbins and Rupert Davies, all of whom became famous actors after the war. He also met the legendary Douglas Bader, who was such a nuisance to the Germans on many occasions, that he had his artificial legs taken away from him. Ken said that Bader used to hide in dustbins and shout rude things at the guards. This made them extremely angry and he was subsequently shipped off to Colditz prison camp, supposedly impossible to escape from. It was interesting that there was a tunnel nicknamed "George" at the theatre, with the trap door access beneath the third seat in the fifth row. It was never used for escaping, but for hiding sand excavated from other tunnels – "Tom", "Dick" and "Harry". One play was called "Alice and her candle", in which men dressed as women. This play was first performed at Dulag Luft, where Wing Commander Harry Day (Wings) was the Senior British Officer. This acting got more vulgar and lewd as the play progressed, so Wings recommended it should not be performed again. The German Camp Commandant who also saw the show commented *"the ladies were too good to be true, or perhaps too true to be good"*.

Theatre was a magic word for prisoners of war, as the weekly visit to it's 400 seater (the seats were made from Red Cross boxes) allowed for the fantasy of escape into the atmosphere of the world they had

CAMP NEWS

MEETING WITH COMMANDANT

At this weeks meeting betweem the S.A.O. & the German Commandant, in the Commandanteur, the following points were raised:-

NO INCREASE IN COAL

It was stated that there w was not the slightest possibility of the ration being increased. Supplies are running short, so Go Easy!

MAIL TO IMPROVE

The S.A.O. enquired into the unusual shortage of mail during the past few weeks & was assured that the position regarding mail would improve considerably in the near future.

PALLIASE COVERS HERE

2000 paper palliase covers ordered by the Germans, have now arrived. These will be issued, in exchange for broken palliase covers.

SALT SOON

Salt will be on the menu, again shortly, we are assured.

CAMP REPAIR SERVICE

The camp repair service is at present busily engaged on the servicing of water jugs & Kein Trinkwasers - when all the u/s ones have been repaired, permission will be sought for the manufacture of certain camp requirements-- cooking utensils, chimmey flues etc.

EDUCATIONAL BOOKS

It is hoped shortly to re-startthe system of interchange of Educational Books, between compounds, parole for this having been given.

HOCKEY

A total of 45 games have been p. played up to & including Jan. 11th S/L Fieldens new no. 2 rink, is now in full operation. An even division of time on the two rinks has been made, giving each team approx. 2 games per week. A total of 55 teams are entered in the league. Games played as follows:- 5 games per day no 1 rink, & 4 per day on no. 2 rink -- 54 games total

S/L Trent the "John L. Lewis" of labour on the rinks has outlined a smooth running programme, in which a block works every 15 days.

CAREFUL WITH STICKS

Approx 65 unbroken sticks remain from the original stock of 145! The season will last as long as the equipment, appeals have been made to the surrounding compounds for loan of kit, The servicing dept is working at full time on the repair of broken sticks, these must be handed in to i/c equipment, present at each game.

Hard working Joe Noble, Bev Smiley, S/L Fielden & Tony Barralet ask your co-operation on the following. Please do not jump over the banks on to the ice during intervals & noon hours for practice. Players only on the rink PLEASE;

SKATE SHARPENER

Sharpemer- arrangements have been made to have a skate sharpener in operation this week., Watch the "HOCKEY" schedule board for details of games to be played.

GIVE YOUR "LIVE·LETTERS" TO YOUR BLOCK "SCANGRIFF" REPRESENTATIVE.

AIR YOUR VIEWS ON ANY SUBJECT THROUGH THE MEDIUM OF THIS COLUMN. YOU CAN MAKE IT REALLY "LIVE"

SCANGRIFF CAMP NEWSPAPER

POW'S DRESSED AS LADIES IN "ALICE AND HER CANDLE" 1943

WHAT'S LEFT OF THE THEATRE IN MARCH 2019.

left behind. The wardrobe was always a challenge, particularly for "ladies" in any show. They had to alter their mannerisms, voices, and practice deportment, until they emerged as good imitations of the glamourous ladies of UK theatre land. Most shows ran for a week, but the POW public was critical and even the camp newspaper, Scandriff, sometimes faintly damned the shows.

Each compound had a fire pool, which was necessary in the event of fire breaking out in the wooden huts. This also doubled as a boating lake in the summer and skating rink in the winter.

In 1943, the Sagan Golf Club was born. It appeared that a POW had got hold of an ancient mashie (like a golf 5 iron) with a hickory shaft. Initially there was just one hole identified with a goal post, which eventually was extended to 18 holes over the camp grounds in north compound. Proper holes were created with old jam tins sunk in the ground. Table tennis was a regular sport and Ken would have excelled at this, in view of his under 18 Warwickshire position pre-war.

North compound had a hospital, which also included a dentist, a cooler for prisoners who had done some misdemeanour (e.g. trying to escape) and a coal store. Adjacent to the entrance was the German guard room and around the perimeter of the camps were seven sentry towers, who would shoot if POWs stepped over the warning wire, which was inside the camp. The coolers were effectively solitary confinement and were quite dank places to be imprisoned even for just 3 weeks (for escaping) and the remains of the cooler floors can still be seen today. Much of the hospital was located underground and serious cases were taken to the nearby Military hospital, which is now Sagan's best hotel!

To the south of the camp was the Appell Ground, where prisoners were required to assemble to be counted twice a day and also to take exercise. There was a marked difference in attitude by the Americans in south compound to those of the British in north. The Americans concluded that it was impossible to avoid having Appells, so would work with the Germans for an orderly assembly. The British however tended to be haphazard. While one group was being counted, others just milled around in their assigned area talking to each other or engaging in horseplay. Some British POWs had been in the camp for many months more than the Americans and their attitude reflected

CAMP LIFE - NOTE THE GOON TOWERS AND FIRE POOL USED AS A BOATING LAKE.

THE CAMP HOSPITAL IN SAGAN, NOW A HOTEL, AS IT IS NOW.

boredom of their predicament, but also an integral part of their escape programme. When a prisoner escaped, the first few hours were crucial because his chances of success increased in proportion to the distance he travelled from the camp, before the alarm was raised. By milling about, the British were able to disguise the absence of someone for a good period of time – much to the annoyance of the Germans.

Each hut had a stove and ingenious POWs created smoke stacks made from Red Cross Klim (powdered milk cans). These Klim tins were also used for air ducting in the tunnels during the Great Escape.

On 16th September 1943, Ken sent a card from Luft 111 to his parents, which arrived in Coventry on 30th October 1943. Ken said:

> *"Dear All, I have moved to another part of the camp now & am sharing a room with 5 other officers – one from Birmingham & one from Leicester. There are several Coventry chaps here and we have long talks about the old town. I am studying various subjects – German, Navigation etc. & find myself fully occupied. The sun has scorched me & I look like a nigger, but am feeling quite fit & well. Please write as often as you can & above all don't worry a scrap – see you soon. Love Kenneth."*

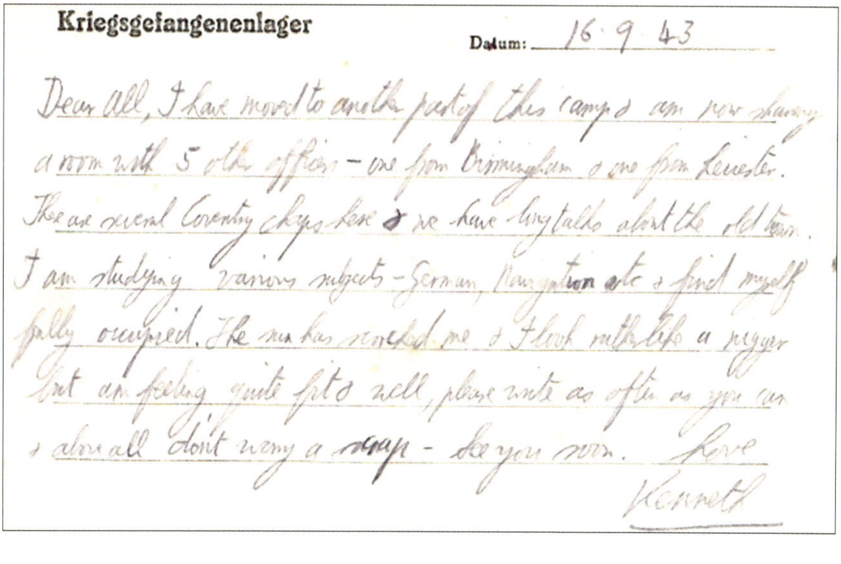

Kriegsgefangenenlager

Datum: 16·9·43

Dear All, I have moved to another part of the camp & am now sharing a room with 5 other officers – one from Birmingham & one from Leicester. There are several Coventry chaps here & we have long talks about the old town. I am studying various subjects – German, Navigation etc & find myself fully occupied. The sun has scorched me & I look rather like a nigger but am feeling quite fit & well, please write as often as you can & above all don't worry a scrap – see you soon. Love Kenneth

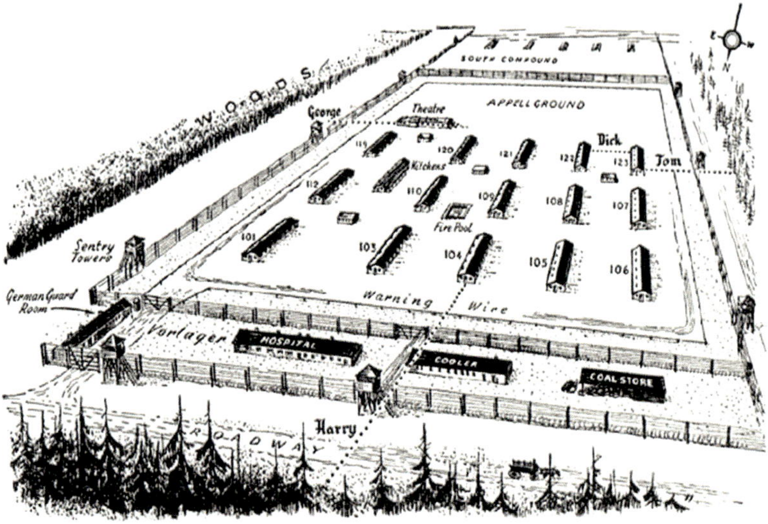

THE NORTH COMPOUND OF STALAG LUFT III

HAUPTMAN PIEBER (ON THE LEFT) SPEAKING WITH THE SENIOR BRITISH OFFICER

Ken had been moved to Hut 112, which housed around 200 POWs. It was on the east side of the northern camp and bordered the fence and trees. Ken's time in camp was quite busy considering the circumstances. He walked 2 miles around the perimeter of the camp (north compound) most days. Prior to the Great Escape he also operated as a "penguin", disposing of sand from tunnels and shuffling it into the earth. A penguin had bags inside his trousers, which contained sand and a string inside that enabled the sand to be disposed of evenly. It seems that there were around 100 penguins in the camp and Ken

KEN ON THE RIGHT WITH FELLOW RAF OFFICES IN HUT 112 IN SEPTEMBER 1943
TAKEN BY HAUPTMAN PIEBER.

HERMAN DEMONSTRATES THE "PENGUIN'S" TROUSER BAGS FOR DISPERSING SAND

(THE BAGS SHOULD BE HANGING INSIDE HIS TROUSER LEGS BUT HE'S WEARING HIS "FERRET" OVERALLS)

RUBBERNECK PLAYS WITH "HARRY'S" AIR PUMP AFTER THE BREAK

commented that wearing these bags meant they were unable to wear underpants. More of this aspect later!

One of the German guards was Hauptmann Pieber, a courteous and mild-mannered man who behaved towards the prisoners in a helpful and friendly manner, in as far as his position allowed. He was an ardent photographer and was keen to take pictures of officers in their room to show that Germans were sensitive. Ken's picture was taken with the other five officers in 1943 and he was permitted to send it home.

The Germans never seemed able to understand the reactions of kriegies either to reprisals or to bad news. It was never as laid down in the Nazi book of rules, and therefore from a German perspective was seen as decadence. The problem for the Germans was that one could pull their legs easily enough, but they would never be able to comprehend the English sense of humour! The same Pieber once walked into a room of kriegies and with a certain amount of ostentatious sympathy said that he was very sorry to advise them that Singapore had "fallen". The kriegie response was "simulated mirth" and one wag said "don't worry Herr Pieber, It's only a loan. It's a trap, you see". Pieber simply couldn't understand the joke!

In a similar vein, on 28th September 1944 the Senior British Officer in north compound posted the following notice:

"Information has been received from the German authorities that certain areas in Germany, in the vicinity of their armament and war industries , have been prescribed in which any unauthorised person is liable to be shot on sight. A request for maps showing these areas has been refused on the grounds that it is undesirable for the German authorities to publish the areas in which their armament industries are situated. Any prisoner of war who escapes or contemplates an escape is advised to avoid such areas if possible."

This notice was publicly displayed, much too the bewilderment of the German staff, who took it very seriously.

It is quite interesting that Ken sent a further card to his parents on 21st September, which also arrived in Coventry on 30th October 1943. Ken said:

"Dear All, I hope my letters etc. are reaching you safely & that you are in good health. I am very fit, but the "novelty" of POW life rapidly wears off. I am looking forward to the day when a cessation of hostilities will enable me to be with you again. I am not worrying however, as I consider myself lucky to have escaped with my life. You can obtain full particulars of parcels, letters etc. from the local Red Cross – please do this.
Keep smiling & hasten the day at the "Cottage".
Love Ken."

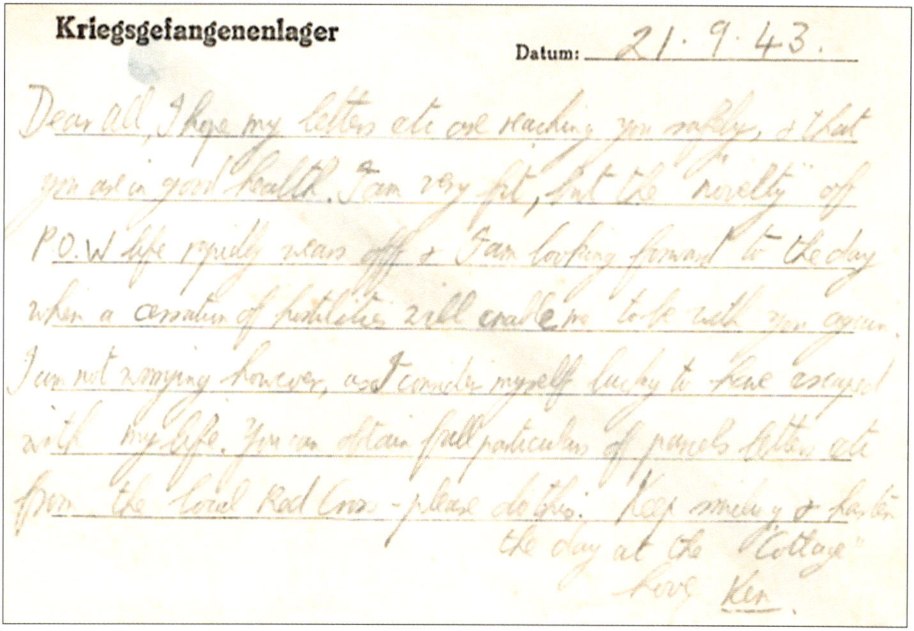
Kriegsgefangenenlager

Datum: 21.9.43.

Dear All, I hope my letters etc are reaching you safely, & that you are in good health. I am very fit, but the "novelty" of P.O.W life rapidly wears off & I am looking forward to the day when a cessation of hostilities will enable me to be with you again. I am not worrying however, as I consider myself lucky to have escaped with my life. You can obtain full particulars of parcels letters etc from the local Red Cross - please do this. Keep smiling & hasten the day at the "Cottage"

Love Ken.

In other cards sent by Ken in September, he requests to be sent toothpaste, underwear /chocolate/ cigarettes (although he didn't smoke), but not food. Ken was rationed to sending 3 letters and 4 cards per month home, although apart from parcels from the UK

ROGER BUSHELL (RIGHT) AT STALAG III AFTER FOUR YEARS ON GERMAN P.O.W. RATIONS, NOT LONG BEFORE THE GREAT ESCAPE. ON THE LEFT IS BATTLE OF BRITAIN ACE, WING COMMANDER BOB TUCK, D.S.O., D.F.C.

(every 3 months) he could receive any number of letters from home.

In a letter home written on 27th October 1943 Ken makes his first reference to church, where he says he read the lesson and specifically states what it was : Isaiah Chapter 21 , where in the text were the words "watchman what of the night" and the answer "the morning comes". Ken says that these words sum up the present situation, for the morning will come sooner than we think. Ken was also issued with a small booklet on The Gospel according to St John. He had this in camp and what was interesting is that he underlined certain passages in it.

On his arrival at the camp he joined the Escape Committee, headed by Squadron Leader Roger Bushell who took the view that prisoners should never tire in their efforts to escape and to "keep the Germans busy". Bushell was head of the escape organisation called X, who was given the nickname "Big X". If they were caught it meant no more than 2 weeks solitary confinement in the cooler – which some actually appreciated surprisingly after sharing a hut with nearly 200 men every day and night. This situation dramatically changed following the 50 murders after the Great Escape.

Many of the bravest escapees were unassuming airmen, who insisted that they had done no more than their duty. For many it was about quiet courage and unquestioned commitment to duty rather than a romantic view of themselves as heroes. The films based on Stalag Luft 111 about the Wooden Horse and the Great Escape had a tendency to glamorise escape, but nothing could be further from the truth.

It is worth briefly mentioning Squadron Leader Roger Bushell, as Ken became quite friendly with him and took it upon himself to communicate with Bushell's parents upon his release. Bushell was an unusual looking chap in an impressive way, that accorded well with his unique personality. He was six foot tall and quite well built. He had remarkable light grey blue eyes that seemed to probe right through you. Born in South Africa, he was a rising London barrister, when war broke out. He joined the Auxiliary Air Force in 1939, but unfortunately was shot down over the beaches at Dunkirk at the end of May 1940. One can fully understand his motivation to escape, having been a prisoner for three years before Ken joined him in August 1943.

After the war Ken wrote some notes under the heading – "why escape" – these included monotony of camp life, food, danger inside camp, length of prison stay. Things they had to consider were tunnelling, what equipment they would need, clothing, forged passes and tools. He also commented that some who had been in the camp for 2/3 years attempted suicide by heading over the perimeter wire, so the German guards would have to shoot them. Some sentries who had lost relatives in bombing of German cities were a little trigger happy and used to take pot shots at any prisoners walking near the wire. This practice was discouraged by the German Camp Commandant, however.

All cards and letters sent from the Camp were intercepted by the censors, as well as books from home to see if any carried "hidden" messages. At Luft 111, there were about one hundred censors – mostly women. Ken certainly had his mail checked, but the censors tended to focus on those they suspected of any activities to do with escaping.

A letter from Yvonne *(whom Ken later married after release)* dated 11th January 1944 that she sent to Ken's parents said how overjoyed she was to receive a box of roses from Ken for Christmas 1943, which he must have organised through the Red Cross. Yvonne used to write to Ken via the Red Cross in Geneva every week and she used to send items, that she thought would be useful to him, to his parents in Coventry to be forwarded in his quarterly parcel.

Ken's father wrote to the British Red Cross on 30th January 1944 asking how Ken could obtain vitamin tablets B, C ,D & F, as Ken says they were very necessary in the camp. His father was not allowed to send them in the quarterly parcels from the UK, so the Red Cross wrote to the Senior Medical Officer at the camp asking for Ken to receive an allocation via their central medical supplies.

A letter was received from Ken (to his parents) on 6th April 1944, and by this time the Great Escape had taken place. In the letter which he had written on 9th January 1944 (taking just over 3 months to arrive), he describes the Christmas celebrations (such as they were) and how much comfort he had taken in the familiarity of the carols sung and how they reminded him of Christmas in better times. Ken says they received some beer but it was non-alcoholic! He also talks of his great love for Yvonne and how he yearns to be back in normal life again. He writes that he would like to thank all who wrote to him in camp but he reserved his 3 letters and 4 postcards per month for the family. A copy of this letter was given to Yvonne.

Mail bound for prisoners was probably the single most important factor in the POW existence. There were no restrictions on the number of letters prisoners could receive from home. Many had to wait 6 months before receiving their first mail from home. The anxieties created by these delays profoundly influenced the tenor of life in camp and added tremendously to the hostile feelings the prisoners held towards the Germans.

At the heart of the prisoners' administrative and organisational system were the military customs and traditions they were all used to. Although they often deviated from the norms of military life in matters of dress, courtesies and personal appearance, they were reacting more to the privations of camp life, than showing a wilful desire to deny their military identities.

CHAPTER 10

The Great Escape and Ken's role

The Great Escape (24th March 1944) is a well-known book and film – made in 1963 starring Steve McQueen, James Garner, Charles Bronson and many other famous actors. Much of the film is accurate, but life being what it was, the actual reality of many aspects of the film are simply untrue. Ken was asked to advise on it. He was not impressed with the result, as the weather was harsh, not spring like (as it is in the film), there were no Americans involved (Steve McQueen and James Garner were included so the film would sell in the American market) and there was no motor bike chase, but as they say, "that's show business!"

So, what was it really like, what happened and how did it come to pass?

There was a very active Escape Committee in the Camp lead by Squadron Leader Roger Bushell, and any planned escapes had to be passed by Roger and the Committee. This was to make sure that their plans were fully supported and didn't clash with any others happening at the same time.

Bushell took the view that it was POWs duty to escape and in mid-1943, he had a vision of a mass escape, which would tie up 1,000s of German troops, who would be looking for them (it was said that at least 100,000 troops would need to be mobilised after any serious breakout). This (in theory) would take them away from front line activity on both the eastern and western Fronts. His vision was to get 200 men out in a single attempt. Many of the POWs didn't share

Bushell's view of the duty of a POW and were opposed to the idea of trying to escape, but went along with the concept, as long as they could carry on as normal, and escaping didn't include them!

Early tunnels were mostly shallow, some being only about three feet deep and many of these were discovered as a result. There was an instance of a horse pulling a ration wagon sticking a hoof through the roof of one tunnel. Faced with a spate of shallow tunnels, the Germans dug a deep trench between the barbed – wire boundary fence and the warning wire to foil tunnelling efforts.

Night and day in all compounds, German security guards patrolled and snooped. These ferrets carried torches and metal spikes. They stooged in and around the huts, probing the ground for tunnels and shining torches in all the dark corners, to try to upset any escape activity, which they thought was happening (which was undoubtedly true).

There were three main tunnels started by the X committee (as mentioned earlier in the story,a fourth was later found underneath

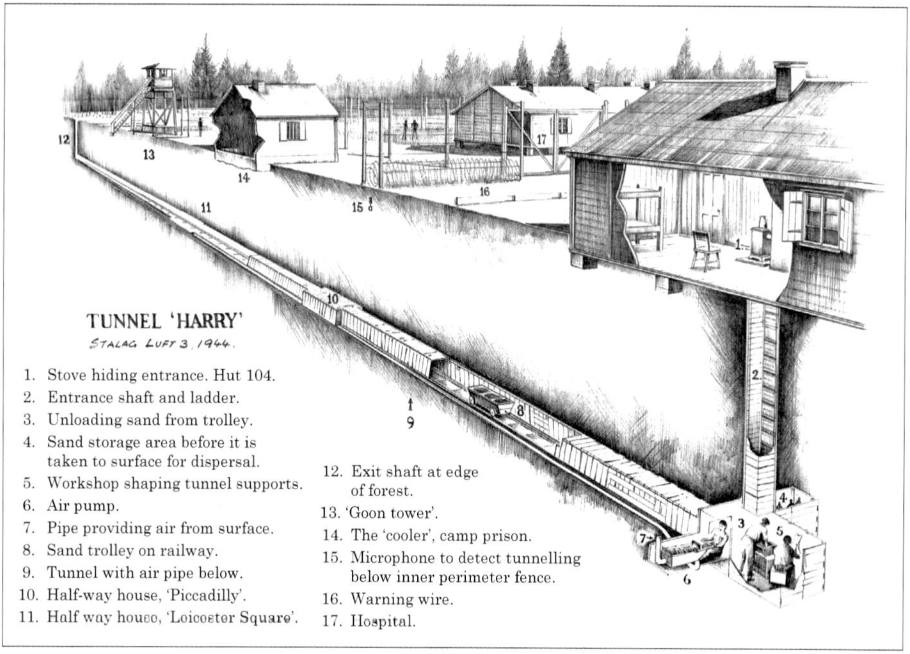

'TUNNEL HARRY' PENCIL DRAWING BY NICOLAS TRUDGIAN. WWW.NICOLASTRUDGIAN.COM

the camp theatre called "George"):

- **"Dick"** was started from Hut 122 and faced west, with its entrance hidden beneath a drain.
- **"Tom"** from Hut 123 also faced west, with its entrance beneath a trapdoor hidden in a dark corner of the hut and adjacent to the perimeter fence. Both Dick and Tom were about 180 feet long and 25ft deep.
- **"Harry"** began from Hut 104 and faced north, with its entrance beneath a stove. When complete "Harry" was 336 ft long and of all the three tunnels, was furthest from the fir trees. It also went under the "cooler" and a sentry box. The advantage of a north exit was that it was nearest to Sagan railway station, so would-be escapers could catch a train and be away from the area quite quickly. Digging out the three tunnels required the disposal of 200 tons of sand and earth, as well as 4,000 bed boards.

The bed boards were needed to shore up the tunnels, as they were built, and each POW was relieved of a number of bed boards for this purpose. Excavation from "Dick" was stopped when the Germans decided to cut down pine trees adjacent to the wire, which allowed them an unrestricted view of the whole camp and so it was too risky to continue.

"Harry" took nearly 12 months to complete and digging ceased for 2 months in January 1944, after discovery of "Tom". "Harry" was an amazing piece of technical ingenuity. Beneath the entrance shaft the POWs created a workshop and installed an air pump constructed from Red Cross tins and bed sheets. The air pump line ran the full length of the tunnel and was made from empty Klim tins. Tunnellers would move on trolleys on wooden railway lines. They passed excavated sand back through the tunnel to the entrance via two "halfway houses"

POW GARDENS WERE STARTED AND SAND DISPERSED INTO THE FLOWER BEDS

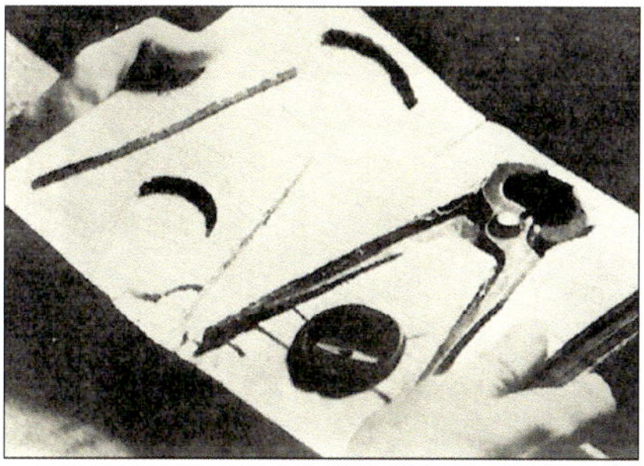

A PAIR OF PINCERS AND ONE OF AL HAKE'S COMPASSES HIDDEN IN A BOOK

which were called "Piccadilly" and "Leicester Square". Originally the tunnellers used candles for light made from the fat from soup with wicks from old or worn clothing, but as progress continued, electric lighting was installed, using stolen electric cable, hooked into the camp's electrical grid. The only issue that occurred was when electricity failed due to Allied bombing of the nearby Sagan station marshalling yard.

Disposal of sand was an ongoing big issue and whilst penguins were able to get rid of some, when the Germans decided to expand

SILK MAP OF GERMANY AND NORTHERN EUROPE

the Camp and covered the proposed exit for Dick, the POWs then used "Dick" to store sand excavated from "Tom" and "Harry".

Another method of sand dispersal was to fill an empty Red Cross cardboard box with sand, join a group sitting around chatting and gradually bury the sand. Perhaps the least stressful way however was during the summer, when sand would be wrapped in a blanket. The blanket laid out on a sandy patch of ground and the carrier would then sunbathe, camouflaging the sand under the blanket at his leisure. These disposal methods were painfully slow, but essential. The tunnellers could dig out sand faster than it could be disposed of, so at times digging was suspended to allow for the surplus to be dealt with satisfactorily. POW gardens were also started and sand dispersed into the flower beds!

Ken was involved in a number of activities in supporting the escape – including operating as a penguin; acting as a look out for guards approaching any huts that were actively digging at the time and drawing maps (silk maps of Germany were sent from Waddingtons in the UK via the food parcels from home – often hidden in book covers). Ken was probably one of the most important people as he could speak German and was engaging with friendly guards who co-operated in supplying railway timetables, maps, civilian clothes and official papers, that were then used to create forgeries.

Some escape tools were sent in parcels from home. For example, POWs were allowed books and hidden inside these were pincers & compasses. Although parcels into the Camp were supposed to be checked by German security, POWs were often used as labour to unload them and contraband would carry some pre-arranged distinguishing mark. Items included such things as cameras, which were considerable help in the forgery of documents and the ability to forge money to produce almost identical replicas to the German Deutsche Mark. Money was delivered into the camp inside phonographic records, along with escape maps and these items would be identified by a spelling error on the record label. There were many designs for escape compasses, but the most popular was the button type which could be worn on uniforms. POWs with experience of making clothes were put to use to create civilian clothing for escapees. These were sometimes old uniforms, but army clothing was supplied in a limited way by the Red Cross, as well as captured army uniforms and boots that had been acquired by the Germans. These POWs secretly created clothing. The workshop under the entrance to the tunnel "Harry", was where they could work, without intrusion.

"Tom" was unfortunately discovered when "goons" noticed ever increasing numbers of penguins go to and from Hut 123 trying to dispose of sand. By chance they found a space, whilst prodding with a rod in the corner of the hut. This was the 98th tunnel to be found in the Camp.

This left "Harry" as the remaining tunnel which was finally ready in March 1944, and although the escape was originally planned for the better weather in the summer, Bushell decided however, that the escape should take place as soon as was practicable. Of the 600 or so POWs who had worked on the tunnels only 200 could be included in the plan. The first 25 were "key players" (good German speakers / main organisers of the Escape – e.g. Roger Bushell) to be out first and the other 175 drew lots. Ken's number was 182, which clearly was to the backend of the escape. Jack Lyons was actually number 79, so he was very lucky not to get out as shall be seen later (Jack died at the age of 101, in 2019).

The escapees had to wait for a moonless night, so they could leave under cover of complete darkness. Bushell decided against delay, as the stove entrance trapdoor to "Harry" had developed a slight wobble, and ferrets were becoming increasingly suspicious of activities in

Hut 104. He decided that to delay a month, until another moonless night, could well have meant the tunnel would have been detected. The forgers were particularly busy on the day prior to the escape, as they had the job of date stamping all papers, notably travel warrants. The date stamps were made inside the camp from rubber boot heels. Finally, on Friday 24th March 1944 the escape attempt began. All involved in the escape were moved to Hut 104 (Ken from Hut 112, for example). By 8pm all escapees were in Hut 104. At 8.30pm Group Captain Martin Massey, the Camp's Senior British Officer entered the block to wish escapers good luck and farewell (interestingly Massey was shortly to be repatriated because of a badly injured leg and looked forward to meeting the successful escapers in London). The tunnel was planned to be opened at 8.45pm, and Leslie Bull was the first man into the tunnel, whose job it was to open the exit shaft. By 9pm everyone was in position in Hut 104, ready to launch what Bushell hoped would be the biggest mass escape in POW history.

In March 1944, the Coventry Telegraph Welfare Record reported "We always remember Kenneth Price, whose inertia while in captivity must be monotonous after his meteoric experiences with the RAF. Little did they know !"

An immediate setback was experienced by heavy snow on the ground and the temperature was well below freezing. The exit trap door to Harry had frozen and freeing it meant a nerve–wracking delay for the 200 escapees in Hut 104.They knew something was amiss, but didn't know what was causing the agonising wait. Just after 9.30pm those near the trap door entrance in the hut felt a sudden blast of icy cold air come shooting out of the tunnel. It had taken over an hour to get the door opened. An even bigger problem was that the exit was 10 feet short of the fir tree line, which would have covered the escape exit! It had been planned that the tunnel would exit in the nearby forest and therefore under cover of the trees.

The first man out emerged at 10.30pm, but since the exit was also a mere fifteen yards from a guard tower, and there was an obvious need to avoid patrolling sentries, the escape was rather slow. With this mishap in terms of the exit hole, Bushell had a brief meeting with others and they decided that rather wait another month to extend

GERMAN FERRET RUBBERNECK HAPPILY DEMONSTRATING WHERE TOM'S TRAP WAS LOCATED.

the tunnel further to the trees, when it might have been discovered, they decided to get as many out immediately, before they were caught. The other big issue was that all the papers were already date stamped. The original plan was for one man out of the tunnel every 2-3 minutes, but this was reduced to ten an hour in view of the problems encountered. Added to these issues, at 11.45pm the sirens suddenly sounded to announce an RAF bombing raid on Sagan station and railway marshalling yards. This meant that the lights in the camp went out everywhere, which of course included the lights in the tunnel. The problems were exacerbated by a small tunnel collapse, which had to be quickly repaired. Those underground were pitched into complete blackness. Fortunately, this possibility had been envisaged and fat lamps kept in the block and down the shafts were brought out and lit. These were passed along the tunnel by stages to the halfway houses. Fat lamps were smelly and dangerous and could only be used at the halfway houses, which meant little or no light in the actual tunnels. At about 2am the lights suddenly came back on again and the "all clear" sounded. The fat lamps were extinguished and the escape operations became easier and less unpleasant. At this point it was decided that they would not achieve their escaper target, so any escapee with a number over 100 would not get out (including Ken). As they were unable to move from Hut 104, they changed back into their uniforms. Had they tried to get back to their own huts, they would have been shot.

At around 4.55am on 25th March, the 77th man was seen emerging from the tunnel by one of the guards, who fired a shot, but was distracted by a shout from an escapee in the fir trees. The bullet went upwards and fortunately missed the 77th man out of the tunnel, who had to surrender. The Germans had no idea as to the entrance location, so this gave time to the remaining escapers to clamber back through the tunnel and join the others who were waiting to destroy their fake papers. Of all the huts in the camp, 104 was the last to be searched, but guards were still unable to find the entrance. In the end a German guard (Unteroffizier Pfelf) crawled the length of the tunnel from outside the wire and then found himself trapped. He called for help and the prisoners opened the entrance to let him out, finally revealing the location.

THE KOMMANDANT, OBERST (COLONEL) VON LINDEINER

Due to the delays in exiting the tunnel and the bombing by the RAF of Sagan Station, many escapees missed their trains and decided to walk towards Czechoslovakia. A number were picked up by the Germans this way, as they were not far enough from the camp, after the escape was discovered. Some of the escapees found that the station entrance was on the other side of the tracks and although there was an entrance on the camp side, they mistook it for an air raid shelter, so passed it by.

CHAPTER 11

The Aftermath

Following the escape, the Germans took an inventory of the camp and found out how extensive the operation had been. The Germans were ruthless even to their own. Electric cable which had been stolen earlier after being left unattended by German workers (used in lighting the tunnel) and they had not reported the theft, so the workers were executed by the Gestapo. From then on, each bed was supplied with only nine bed boards, which were counted regularly by guards.

Understandably, the camp Commandant Colonel Von Lindeiner was furious. He was a highly decorated WW1 veteran and a former member of Goering's personal staff when WW2 broke out. He was well educated, spoke excellent English and had the respect of the senior Allied officers in the camp. He had joined the Luftwaffe, as it was the armed service most independent of the Nazis. He tried to follow the rules laid out by the Geneva Convention, but was thwarted on direct orders of Hitler.

After discovery of the escape, all those in Hut 104 (including Ken) were paraded without coats and trousers in the snow to take part in a complete photographic identity check. After two hours they were marched over to the compound gate. Undoubtedly the Germans wanted to put them all in the cooler, but there just wasn't room, so eventually the men were returned to their own blocks.

During his regime at the camp, the Commandant instigated weekly conferences between the Senior British Officer and German senior staff. This practice ceased after the Great Escape.

Von Lindeiner was sixty- one years old when he was appointed Commandant at Stalag Luft 111 in May 1942. He was a staunch German, but had no affection for the Nazi regime. He had wanted to retire, but the authorities wouldn't let him go. In all the time during his tenure at the camp, he tried to keep the Secret Service (SS) from interfering. This all changed after the Great Escape. He wore an Iron Cross first class and was reputedly an Aide to the Kaiser in the last war (WW1). He was certainly due for promotion to general on two occasions, but these were thwarted by two mass escapes, that were staged from north compound at crucial moments.

For allowing this escape, Von Lindeiner was sent to the eastern Front (which was regarded as a death sentence). He was injured twice, but survived the war.

In terms of the 76 that got out, they were up against it from the start, due to the black out and difficulty in finding their way to Sagan railway station. Trains were disrupted due to Allied bombing, so many of the escapees missed their planned trains and their onward connections. While the flap was going on in the camp after the discovery, many of those who had got out of the tunnel were making good headway on their journeys. This brisk progress did not last however, because in a matter of hours the whole countryside was roused and out searching for them, in what was to be one of the biggest man hunts in Germany throughout the war. Thousands of Germans were engaged in this search and to this end Roger Bushell had achieved one of his objectives in tying up German personnel in the search, rather than fighting the Allies. 73 escapees were caught in a matter of days, but three – two Norwegians and a Dutch man did make it back to the UK. Information, brought into camp by guards, indicated that an amazing figure of 5 million Germans had to spend some of their time looking for the prisoners. This in itself made the escape, in one respect, a considerable success, because these attempts cause the diversion of part of the enemy's manpower.

A few days after the break- out, a team of Gestapo and SS men descended on the camp to investigate the affair, at which point the Commandant and the German Chief Security Officer took to their beds, allegedly ill. Neither the Gestapo or SS were popular with ordinary German troops, so when the Gestapo made a very thorough search of north compound they had no help from the German guards. Had the Gestapo discovered anything of importance, it would have reflected badly on the German ferrets. They found nothing, other than uncovering a black market run by the Commandant – where wines and foods were flown in from Denmark. This led to the speedy court martial of the Commandant and other senior German officers.

Hitler initially wanted all the escapees to be shot as an example to other prisoners, as well as Von Lindeiner, the Camp Security Officer and the guards on duty at the time. Herman Goering, Field Marshall Keitel and Major General Von Graevenitz (who was in charge of POWs) all argued against any executions as a violation of the Geneva Convention. Hitler relented and instead ordered Himmler (Head of the SS) to execute more than half of the escapees. Fifty were shot (murdered) on the pretext of resisting arrest or making further attempts to escape after arrest. These included Roger Bushell, but none of the 50 seemed to have sustained injuries. It appears that the re-captured prisoners were killed in small groups by Gestapo officers – most often shot in the back of the head during toilet breaks, when they were supposedly being driven back to the camp. Clearly at the time the Germans (notably the Gestapo) were keen to cover up these atrocities. All the bodies were immediately cremated and there was some delay in acknowledging their deaths. Even the Camp authorities could not explain why there were no injuries to any of the 50.This would seem plausible if the escapees were running, they might have been hit by bullets, but not necessarily shot dead – just sustaining injuries. 23 escapees were returned to camp to spend three weeks in the cooler. For a short period of time following the escape, the camp was run by the Gestapo, before returning it's running to the Luftwaffe.

Although Ken didn't tell the author, he did mention to David Oldcorn a near neighbour in Iver after the war that the 23 who were returned to camp and those, including Ken, who didn't get out of the tunnel, felt guilty for "surviving".

The new Commandant was Oberstleutnant (Lieutenant Colonel)

Korda, who seemed fairly inconspicuous and kept himself to his quarters most of the time. As he felt the escape had little to do with him, he did not seek extreme reprisals. He shut the camp theatre and did not allow the POWs to keep Red Cross boxes or old food tins. Also for a short while, he held three appels a day. Even after two weeks there was still no news of the escapees who hadn't been returned to camp. Suddenly Hauptmann Pieber called Group Captain Massey, the Senior British officer to meet the Commandant, together with Massey's interpreter. The Commandant said that he been told by "his higher authority" to communicate this report: *"The Senior British Officer is to be informed that as a result of the tunnel in which 76 officers escaped from Stalag Luft 111, north compound, 41 of these officers have been shot while resisting capture or attempting escape, after arrest"*. Massey simply couldn't believe what he had heard and couldn't understand why none were wounded. The Commandant simply said that he was advised not to answer questions. All the Commandant offered was to let Massey have the names of those shot. Massey also wanted to know what had happened to the bodies, so he could arrange burial and disposal of their effects. The Commandant said he would let Massey have any scrap of information, as soon as he was informed.

German crimes were already well known and documented, with the ongoing murder of Poles, Czechs and Russians whom they regarded as "lower beings". This on top of the long drawn out massacre of Jews. The cold-blooded butchery of British prisoners of war opened a new chapter in the grimy history of German atrocities during WW2.

On hearing the news, Massey summoned the senior officer in every hut (which included Ken in Hut 112) to the camp theatre for him to make the announcement about the shootings. He reported in turn that 41 had been shot, as he had been told, although subsequently, it turned out there were 50 in total.

After a while the Germans brought back the personal belongings of the missing 50 and a short while later they brought in urns carrying the cremated ashes of those who had been killed. The case against the Germans was obvious, in that they had been cremated to destroy the evidence of the manner of death.

As mentioned before, there were mixed views over the escape. From those in the camp at the time, who didn't wish to "rock the boat" and get out, and those who felt that it was a POWs duty to try to escape.

The Germans issued a poster saying it wasn't a duty to try to escape and this poster made it clear how such escapes would be dealt with!

Many (including those who didn't take part in the escape) have subsequently said (quoting an unnamed POW) - *"I sometimes think it wasn't worth it. 50 mens' lives it cost to tie up those Germans. Inevitably they would have lost the war – and 50 people would have been alive today"*. Jack Lyons view on the cost in lives was that it had to be looked at in perspective - just a week later the RAF lost 90 aircraft and 500 men in a raid on Nuremberg.

Recent documents (July 2021) found in the National Archives suggest that the Nazi leaders knew about the Great Escape in advance and let it go-ahead, because they wanted to make an example of the ringleaders. After the break-out, Henrich Himmler could then use the escape to cold-bloodedly hunt down the brave airmen. These documents also suggest that in November 1943, a thorough inspection by the SS at the camp concluded that there was no more tunnelling and ordered that the microphones be switched off for a three week period. The muting of microphones for this length of time was a remarkable step, in view of the known tunnelling activities. According to the files, Von Lindeiner, Camp Commandant protested at this action and said an escape was imminent and he feared the consequences. His fears were borne out after the Great Escape. Personally, I find these claims hard to substantiate, as POW intelligence gathering was very good and I think they would have known what the Germans were doing.

The Prisoner of War News was published monthly by the Red Cross in London and there is a report in August 1944 from Sir Anthony Eden, Foreign Secretary in the War Time Government, under the heading : The Shooting of Prisoners. *On the plea that Mr Eden made "unheard –of allegation" that 50 officers who escaped from Stalag Luft 111 were murdered , the Nazi Government have refused a Berlin broadcast to make a further report on the matter*. The broadcast adds that the country which began the bombing on civilians has no moral right to speak in this matter, let alone make accusations. Comment

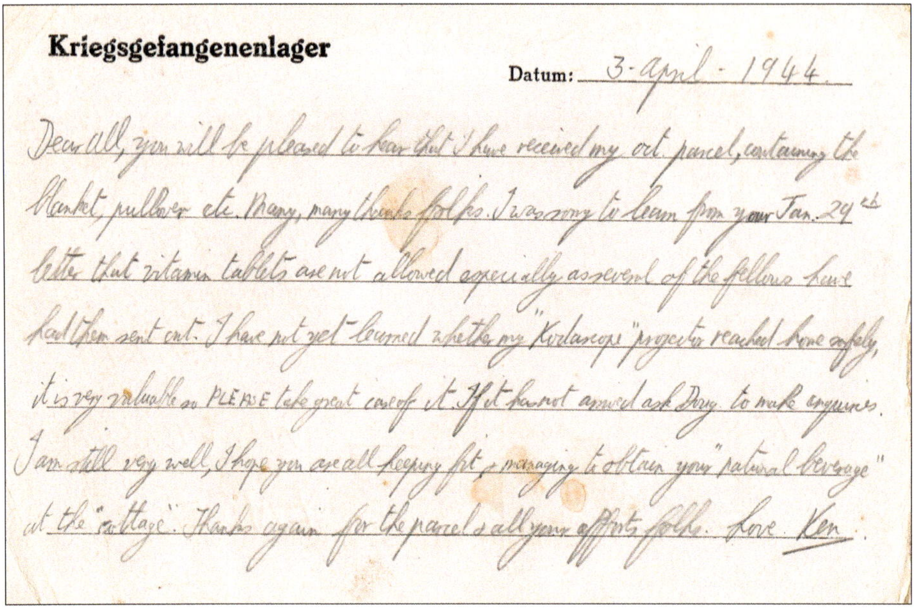

Kriegsgefangenenlager

Datum: 3 - April - 1944.

Dear All, you will be pleased to hear that I have received my oct. parcel, containing the blanket, pullover etc. Many, many thanks folks. I was sorry to learn from your Jan. 29th letter that vitamin tablets are not allowed especially as several of the fellows have had them sent out. I have not yet learned whether my "Kodascope" projector reached home safely, it is very valuable so PLEASE take great care of it. If it has not arrived ask Doug. to make enquiries. I am still very well, I hope you are all keeping fit & managing to obtain your "natural beverage" at the "cottage". Thanks again for the parcel & all your efforts folks. Love Ken

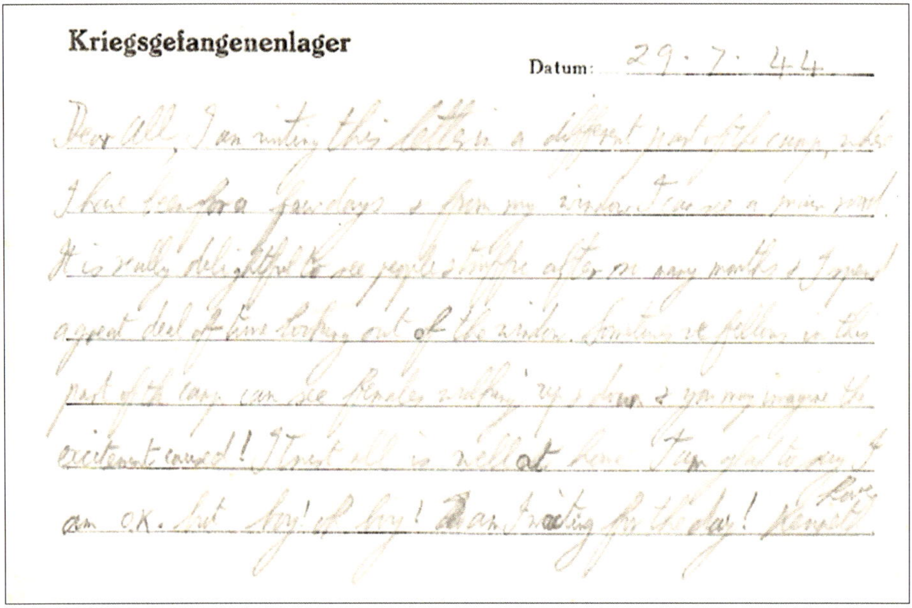

Kriegsgefangenenlager

Datum: 29 · 7 · 44

Dear All, I am writing this letter in a different part of the camp, where I have been for a few days & from my window I can see a main road. It is really delightful to see people & traffic after so many months & I spend a great deal of time looking out of the window. Sometimes we fellows in this part of the camp can see females walking up & down & you may imagine the excitement caused! I trust all is well at home. I am glad to say I am O.K. but boy! oh boy! Am I waiting for the day! Love Kenneth is superfluous. A recent announcement was made of the shooting at other camps of another 23 prisoners. It appears that these incidents appeared at different times since August 1943 and at different camps. There has been, so far as is known, no repetition of any such occurrence as that which took place at Stalag Luft 111.

Time in Stalag Luft 111 after the escape was frightening and stressful, as the Germans were thereafter ever watchful for future escape activities.

On 3rd April 1944, Ken sent a card from Luft 111 to his parents, which arrived in Coventry on 17th July 1944. Ken said:

"Dear All, you will be pleased to hear that I have received my October parcel, containing the blanket, pullover etc. Many, many thanks folks. I was sorry to learn from your Jan 24th letter that vitamin tablets are not allowed especially as several of the fellows have had them sent out. I have not yet learned whether my "Kodascope" projector reached home safely. It is very valuable so PLEASE take great care of it. If it has not arrived ask Doug to make enquiries. I am still very well. I hope you are all keeping fit & managing to obtain your natural beverage at the Cottage. Thanks again for the parcel & all your efforts folks. Love Ken."

It was interesting that this card was written just ten days after the escape and with the camp in mourning Ken makes no reference to it. Had he done so, almost certainly the German censor would have put a black line through any reference or it may have been that the card would not have been sent. POWs, in communicating home, had to be seen to be appearing upbeat about their treatment by the Germans.

On 29th July 1944, Ken sent a card from Stalag Luft 111 to his parents, which arrived in Coventry on 20th November 1944. Ken said:

"Dear All, I am writing this card in a different part of the camp, where I have been for a few days & from my window I can see a main road. It is really delightful to see people & traffic, after so many months. I spend a great deal of time looking out of the window.

Sometimes we fellows in this part of the camp can see females walking up & down & you can imagine the excitement caused! I trust all is well at home. I am glad to say I am ok. But boy! Oh boy! Am I waiting for the day! Love Kenneth."

Ken doesn't say anymore, other than we assume he was referring to the day when he gets home safely.

In October Ken talks about hearing that his old friends from the RAF station at Wyton were getting married to WAAFs and producing babies by the score. He says that he will be well behind in that race, but would make up for it when he gets out of camp. He was concerned

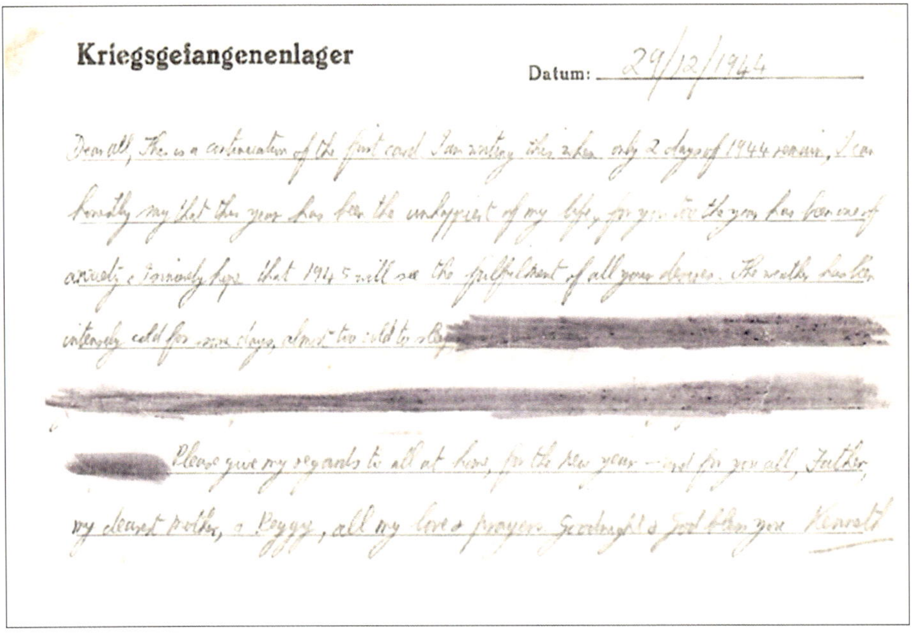

Kriegsgefangenenlager

Datum: 29/12/1944

Dear all, This is a continuation of the first card I am writing this when only 2 days of 1944 remain, I can honestly say that this year has been the unhappiest of my life, for you too the year has been one of anxiety & I sincerely hope that 1945 will see the fulfilment of all your desires. The weather has been intensely cold for some days, almost too cold to sl[redacted] Please give my regards to all at home, for the New year — and for you all, Father, my dearest Mother, & Peggy, all my love & prayers. Goodnight & God bless you Kenneth

that Yvonne did not see or hear that comment though. He slightly morbidly suggests that he doesn't know if she will have him yet, as he says he is a "pretty bad type", suggesting perhaps that he felt he wasn't "good enough" for Yvonne.

In a letter home in September 1944 Ken makes reference to the invasion of Normandy in June that year, which interestingly was missed by the German censor.

On 29th December 1944, Ken sent a card from Luft 111 to his parents, which arrived in Coventry on 3rd February 1945. In the letter Ken said:

"Dear All, This is a continuation of the first card. I am writing this when only 2 days of 1944 remain. I can honestly say that this year has been the unhappiest of my life. For you too, the year has been one of anxiety. I sincerely hope that 1945 will see the fulfilment of all your desires. The weather has been intensely cold for some days, almost too cold to sleep (note here the German censor must have deleted something Ken had written). Please give my regards to all at home, for the New Year – and for you all, Father, my dearest mother & Peggy, all my love & prayers. Good night & God bless you. Kenneth."

At this time boredom, monotony and uncertainty about their fate with the war going against the Germans and whether they would be murdered or used as human shields were a great burden on POWs and Ken was no exception. It was an interesting comment Ken made in a letter home on 12th June 1944 saying that some of his fellow POWS had received letters from home accusing them of cowardice for sheltering in a POW camp. Ken was very unhappy about these comments and went on to say (using space in his letter to do so) that from his experience it takes a particularly strong man to endure being a POW, rather than to face untold dangers in war.

CHAPTER 12

The Long March

Towards the end of 1944 it was clear that the Germans would eventually lose the war, but there was no certainty as to when. The Axis forces had been kicked out of North Africa by Montgomery. The Russians had turned the tables on the Germans at Stalingrad and were fast advancing west. The Allies had invaded Normandy in northern France in June and were advancing east and the Italians had surrendered, and switched sides to the Allies.

THE LONG MARCH

Sagan was in the east of Poland and with the Russians advancing quickly, it was clear that camp would be liberated in a matter of days by the end of January 1945. The Germans therefore faced a challenge of how to deal with the POWs. Hitler was conscious of the impending problem, and on 19th July 1944, a day before his assassination attempt, he issued orders for the "Defence of the Reich". Within these orders was the decision to evacuate the POWs in the eastern areas of Poland and Germany to Saxony and northern areas around Lubeck and Hamburg. This began the events of the "Long March" in the latter part of January 1945.

At this time, prisoners concluded that there were several contingencies for which they should be prepared.

These included:

- A German withdrawal, that would leave prisoners on their own.
- An attempt by the Germans to move them into cities to discourage Allied bombing or into a redoubt after which the Germans would bargain for peace terms, using POWs as hostages.
- A move westwards before the Russian Army.
- A rescue attempt by Allied forces or envelopment by advancing Russians and finally an attempt by the Germans to liquidate them "en masse".

As it turned out, it was the march westwards was the answer – hence the "Long March".

In January 1945 (undated due to the German censor) Ken sent a letter home saying how conditions in the camp were deteriorating, but most were quite positive about release quite soon. He went on to say that an Australian friend of his in camp (who was badly injured when his plane was shot down in January 1944) was being repatriated to the UK (in an exchange for an injured German) and would be making contact with his parents. It was clear that Ken hadn't received much post in recent months, as he made reference to asking how his "darling" Yvonne was. This heavily censored letter was received in Coventry on 25th April 1945.

At 9.30pm on Saturday 27th January 1945, the order was given to evacuate the camp with just 30 minutes notice. In reality, the POWs finally paraded at 12.15am on Sunday 29th January. This lucky delay gave them time to make sledges to tow their kit, enabling them to carry much more. Everything from coal boxes to Red Cross arm chairs went into making these items. Ken was part of this event. Each POW was initially instructed to bring only what he could carry, so accumulated books and other heavy items had to be abandoned. Each man was issued with a Red Cross parcel, but in most cases they were too heavy to carry and so the POWs took only the dry rations. There was very little transport, other than a few horse-drawn carts for those were too ill to walk. It was one of the coldest winters on record at -20 degrees centigrade, with thick snow and ice all around. They eventually left the camp at 5am for a 12 mile trek to a small village called Kunau. Ken reckons he survived by wearing an oil filled sweater that his parents sent from home, which thankfully kept him warm. Many years later he was still seen wearing this, whilst gardening at home in Iver.

In March 1945, the Coventry Telegraph Welfare Record had little information on Ken and simply stated that *"as far as we are able to ascertain he is still a prisoner of war in Germany"* – they knew nothing about the "Long March".

Rumours had spread across the north compound about why they were being moved. These ranged from the idea that the Germans were using POWs as human shields to the fear that they were to be gassed by the SS – knowledge of the Holocaust was widespread by 1945!

About 30,000 POWs were forced to march approximately 70 miles in dreadful conditions, with little food, water or accommodation. Most had to bed down on the snow, although some did find stables with straw to keep warm. Hundreds died of starvation, disease, exhaustion or malnutrition and it is known that at least 4,000 had dysentery, flu and frostbite. There were reports of some resorting to eating dogs, cats, rats and grass, they were so hungry. From the gates of Stalag Luft 111, the POWs marched through the wooded countryside of

Silesia and towards Berlin. After 12 miles, they reached their first stop a small Polish town called Ilowa. 500 of them were lucky enough to find sanctuary in the local church. Many of the German guards were in worse shape than the POWs because generally they were a good deal older and were unsuitable for front line combat. Most were WW1 veterans – nearly 30 years previously.

They stopped at various hamlets and towns enroute, staying in barns and abandoned factories, hunting for food and trying the best they could to survive, under the appalling conditions. It was a fight for survival. Many POWs were broken up into groups of 250-300 men, because of the inadequate roads and flow of the battle. Not all prisoners followed the same route. The locals reacted in different ways – passing through some villages, the residents would throw bricks and stones at the prisoners, and in others they would share their last food. Some POWs who tried to escape were shot by guards – which under the Geneva Convention was allowed.

Ken reported that many were exhausted, hungry and delirious with the cold and lead to many of his colleagues collapsing by the roadside. He went on to say that the only way to march without getting your head frozen was to bend at the waist, twist your shoulders and bow your head into the teeth of the freezing gale. No-one spoke, saving all their energy for their legs. Occasionally they were passed by a horse-drawn cart with flattened stiff bodies on it. These were clearly POWs, who had died earlier in the march. He also said that so little water was issued, that men drank snow or water from the ground or from ditches that others had used as latrines – a very unhealthy thing to do, but they were desperate! On 2nd February after 70 miles, they arrived at a railhead called Spremberg, where they were billeted in 8th Panzer Division's reserve depot.

Ken said that German propaganda preyed on prisoners' minds – be it that they would never see their wives and sweethearts again or that they should switch sides to join the Germans fighting the Russians. Or even that the SS would shoot them all.

There was one occasion when the marching POWs were caught in what is known as "friendly fire". The column was at a village called Gresse, when they were mistakenly strafed by a group of RAF Hawker

Typhoons (fighters) who didn't know that they were RAF POWs. 60 sadly lost their lives in this fire and it caused many to escape into ditches to hide from the attack.

At Spremberg, the POWs were divided up into cattle trucks and railway cars and spent 3 months being transported over Germany. Either going east as the Allies advanced or west away from the Russian advance. During that time, the weather improved, although the food, as ever, was in very short supply. On 2nd May 1945 Ken finished up in Trenthorst, 12 miles from Lubeck on the Baltic coast. Ken sent a letter home which arrived on 7th May and the author highlighted extracts from it, to demonstrate his feelings which are shown below:

"This is probably the first news you have received from me for some time. Today British tanks burst in on us and we are free men again!!! I have heard no news from you since last November (1944), and I guess news from me is equally scarce. I will never forget this day after watching & hearing a battle south of here for some days, the armoured cars & tanks drove in today – I almost kissed the driver of the car – a Lieutenant from the Cheshire Regiment!"

It was later estimated that many of the POWs had walked over 500 miles by the time they were liberated and some as much as one thousand miles.

The author has a copy of the RAF Standing orders dated 1st May 1945, for officers who were based at Trenthorst, which for many, was almost like being in prison camp again. It gives details of times in their billets, where they should sleep, and that there must be no smoking in barns or cow sheds. Also, where personnel should relieve themselves and interestingly, that all will respect German personnel and property.

On 4th May 1945, RAF Bomber Command implemented Operation Exodus and over the next month they flew 2,900 sorties to repatriate 75,000 prisoners of war.

The war ended on 8th May 1945 and Ken was repatriated to the UK on 3rd June 1945. In the interim a Luftwaffe officer surrendered his

Luger (pistol) to Ken, which Ken kept (with 200 rounds of ammunition) in his desk in Iver, until his death in April 1980. At the time there was a lot of publicity about WW2 veterans keeping memorabilia and instead of having the gun demobilised, his son (author) threw both the gun, holster and ammunition into a local canal, where we assume it still rests.

Sadly, Ken never saw his mother Harriet again. She died on 20th February 1945, when he was still a prisoner of war. Ken's father George chose not to tell Ken about her death, as he (rightly) felt he didn't want to impart negative/sad thoughts to him at the time. Ken only learnt of her death when he returned to the UK in June 1945 and was able to visit the cemetery in Coventry. She was only 60 years old and had been suffering from cancer.

CHAPTER 13

Ken's early years after release from POW Camp

Ken remained in the RAF as a Wing Commander from June 1945 until April 1946, where he was based at Transport Command Head Quarters. He married his true love and sweetheart, Yvonne Randall in Exeter on 21st June 1946 and in their early years, they lived in a flat in Putney, West London.

KGP & YMP June 1946 - tif

On his return home, he was issued with a booklet by the Air Ministry for ex-prisoners of war called "Going on Leave". It is worth dwelling on this booklet for a moment as it gives a fascinating insight into what "kriegies" could expect when they got home. The Air Ministry referred to ex POW's as kriegies in the booklet.

The booklet covered a number of topics and under the heading *"So this is Britain"*, it informed the newly repatriated POW: *"You will find that many changes will have taken place whilst you were incarcerated". It particularly says that "people stand in queues waiting for their turn to be served with rations of meat or groceries. The trains are usually packed, because many have been taken off owing to war traffic. It all needs good humour – so get it ready and don't let your own war weariness get you or your friends down".* It also points out that it is a well-worn joke nowadays that the customer, not the shop, is always wrong.

Nothing much has changed since then!

The first "port of call" for a POW was a Reception Centre, where they were given 28 days immediate leave after filling in forms and

KEN AND YVONNE ON THEIR WEDDING DAY ON 21ST JUNE 1946.

meeting the Medical Officer. They were then issued with ration cards, which allowed them to purchase food at double those rations applicable to civilians. As they couldn't buy sweets and tobacco in confectioners, they had to source these via the local NAAFI (it stands for Navy, Army and Air Force Institutes) and is the forces retail shop. The Reception Centre also issued clothing coupons to officers – which was 88 coupons per year. A pair of shoes, for example, was 9 coupons and a shirt - 5 coupons. This allowance didn't last very long, so the booklet advised officers to buy second hand at Station (based on camp)

Equipment stores.

They were also allowed to claim for any expense incurred whilst escaping, which was challenging as this had to be validated. There is no record of Ken having made any claim.

In their first 28 days of leave, they were allowed 300 miles of recreational motoring – not much use to Ken, as he hadn't got a driving licence. He didn't pass his test until the late 1950s.Yvonne (his wife) did all the driving up to that point.

On arrival at the Reception Centre Ken was given £10 advance of pay and issued with an Identity card. The booklet says *"that the ex POW will be astonished that after five years of war there is still such a variety of food. It goes on to say that there are shortages, chiefly of imported foodstuffs, but you will be surprised how successfully your womenfolk have managed to overcome the difficulties".*

The "So this is Britain" booklet made the point that fuel for heating was in short supply, so the ex POW would be doing less than his duty if he complained about the cold. They were also restricted to no more than 5 inches of water in the bath. They were also advised to get a booklet from the Reception Centre, if they were planning to go on leave to London. Arrangements had been made for officers to use accommodation provided by a selection of hotels in town. If using public transport, officers had to be in uniform and were issued with a 48 hour travel pass for one shilling (approximately 8 pence in today's money).

The booklet advises that Station life will have changed to the extent that there are a large number of WAAF (Women's Auxiliary Air Force) now doing work which used to be done by men. Many aircraft are checked by airwomen fitters and riggers. Leave is allocated on the basis of seven days every quarter, which includes a free travel warrant. Officers are allowed one day per week off their base.

It further contained a lengthy piece on air force welfare, which included guidance on living conditions, personal worries, legal aid in the event of divorce and where to go for financial help in the period before returning to civilian life.

Concluding in quite a colloquial manner, the booklet says: *"Well, that's the gen. You'll probably have many other questions to ask*

YEAR 1943-44, ENDING 5 APRIL, 1944

	£	s.
From Official Emoluments	448	
From		
Total	448	

DEDUCTIONS FOR—

	£	s.
VA	28	
Allowance for earned income	42	
Personal allowance	80	
Wife's earned income allowance		
Housekeeper		
Children		
Dependent relatives		

	£	s.
(Total deductions)	150	
Net amount chargeable to tax	298	
Amount on which tax is chargeable at 6/6 in the £	165	
Balance chargeable at the standard rate of 10/- in the £	133	

	£	s.	d.
TAX CHARGEABLE at 6/6 in the £	53	12	6
TAX CHARGEABLE at 10/- in the £	66	10	
	120	2	6

Deduct from the above Tax :—
Allowance for Life Assurance

	£	s.
£ 1 @ 5/- in the £		5
£ @ / in the £		

	£	s.	d.
(Deduction)		5	
NET TAX PAYABLE	119	17	6
Tax payable as previously notified	76	2	6
Increase/Decrease	43	15	—

NOTES

Tax Deducted £ 76 · 2 · 6

Under Collection c/f 1944/45 £ 43 - 15 - 0.

besides. If so, tackle the Welfare Officers at the Reception Centres – they're there to advise you."

As an aside to this advice, in spite of the fact that Ken had been a POW for nearly 2 years, he received a letter from "Assessors of Income Tax" stating that he owed the Inland revenue £43.15 shillings covering the years of 1943 to end April 1945. It seems amazing that even when he was incarcerated by the Germans, he still had to pay income tax!

On the reverse of the booklet, Ken had made some fairly illegible pencil notes, but the author was able to discern that he needed to write to Mr and Mrs Bushell as he owed them a £1.00 for getting Yvonne her birthday present on 21st June 1945 (the Bushells' son led the Great Escape). He also needed to write to his sister Peggy advising of his release, visit Coventry and answer correspondence.

CHAPTER 14 -

Ken - 1946 onwards Life in Peacetime.

SG TAKOB WACHOWIAKSS 1943

In chapter 4, I referred to Sg Takob Wachowiak of the SS who had “rescued” Ken from the Gestapo in August 1943. On 13th November 1947, Ken was forwarded a letter sent to the War Office by Wachowiak, saying that he was being held by the Canadians in Holland on “alleged” war crimes. In the letter, Wachowiak makes reference regarding interceding to get Ken’s release into a “normal” POW camp.

He goes on to say that Major Price assured him about his good treatment and handed his address to him, mentioning he could use it at some point. Wachowiak lost the address, hence he wrote to Ken via the War Office. There is no record of any response from Ken, although the family believe he didn't reply and felt he had been tricked at the time of his release from the Gestapo anyway.

In April 1946, Ken was demobilised and joined the Ministry of Civil Aviation on 26th April, as an Operations Officer Grade 2, where he was mainly responsible for planning and policy on navigation aids and air traffic control. He was awarded his Certificate of qualifying as an Operations Officer on 10th September 1948. In 1952 he was promoted to Operations Officer Grade 1, where his work involved international air traffic control and navigation techniques. In 1964, he was again promoted to Deputy Director, Operations with the Ministry of Civil Aviation. He had a multiplicity of responsibilities concerned with civil aviation, which included flying clubs, aerodrome planning and looking at airspace requirements within the UK. He was now also the UK representative in Brussels on Eurocontrol, where he represented the UK at approximately 30 international civil aviation meetings. In 1957, he was also seconded to the Danish Government for a month to advise on air traffic control matters, which Ken sorted to the satisfaction of the Danes. He was also responsible for flight crew licensing and & supervision of commercial schools at Hamble, Oxford, Perth and Carlisle.

For most of his time with the Ministry of Aviation, he was based in some bland offices in Tavistock Square in Central London. In March 1964, he was appointed as Deputy Director of Operations in the Southern Division of the Ministry of Aviation, based at Heston in West London.

We learnt in recent years, that he was one of 5,000 civil servants destined for underground bunkers in the event of a nuclear war, which in the 1960s and 1970s was very much in peoples' minds.

In June 1978, at the age of 58, he took early retirement on health grounds. His health had never really recovered from his time as a prisoner of war (1943- 1945). He suffered from ulcerative colitis in the 1960s and had to be on a wide range of pills for the rest of his life. He was diagnosed with bowel cancer in 1979 and sadly lived just another year, before he died in April 1980.

He lived in Iver, Bucks all his life and moved there from Putney, West London in 1947. He had three children – Alistair (the author) in 1948, Malcolm in 1952 and Wendy in 1955. He lived for his family, but was very involved in the local community. He was Chairman of the Richings Park (part of Iver) Residents Association between 1953 and 1959 and at the same time also Chairman of the local Youth club, Scout Supporters group and the local Girl Guides. He was also a member of the Parochial Church Council. In addition, he was the Richings Park correspondent for the Slough Express newspaper for 26 years. He was paid an old penny per line for what was printed and this role did require him to maintain many contacts with visits to local hostelries on a regular basis! He also enjoyed writing, gardening, tennis, bridge, walking, the National Trust and vintage aircraft.

Ken loved writing and in 1955 together with a friend in Iver – Len Naylor – who did the illustrations, he wrote a children's book called Ronald the Rapide. This was based on a de Havilland DH 89 Dragon Rapide - a 1930s short haul biplane that could accommodate 6-8 passengers. It proved an economical and durable aeroplane, despite it's relatively primitive plywood construction. Ronald came to life in the book and had a great affinity with children and was always competing with Cyril the Comet and Sydney the Stratocruiser. Ken's disappointment was that the book and four others, he had planned, were never published. He felt that the concept was later used to create other books, based on humanised mechanical characters, which became very successful.

In 1958, Ken also wrote an extensive study on Air Traffic Control in the UK, which was entitled "Highways of the Air – the Air Traffic Control Story" . He talks about the fact that transport of passengers and freight by air only really began in 1919 after WW1 and in 1955, 65,000 flights were made across the Atlantic between Europe and the USA, carrying over 7 million people. The key point which Ken develops is that transport of all forms needed to be regulated and he goes to show in depth about how these controls developed after WW2. He submitted his manuscript with pictures and drawings to Ernest

Benn Ltd, publishers in London in October 1958, only to receive a response on 31st October that year saying they did not feel it would be suitable for their list, as it was lacking any wide interest. Ken was understandably disappointed, and the book was never published.

I don't think Ken had a great deal of religious faith after his time as a POW, and it wasn't until he was very ill in the Central Middlesex Hospital in 1962 that things changed. The medical profession at the time, felt it had stemmed for his time in prisoner of war camp. He had a visit from the Reverend Wellandar, who was then vicar of Iver and subsequently became Bishop of Liverpool. Wellandar told Ken that he wasn't going to die, as God had an important role for him. This was to launch Christian Stewardship to 600 people at an event at Heathrow Airport. This Ken made this presentation and Stewardship is now the norm for most Church of England churches.

In 1976 Ken wrote to the Ministry of Defence about his medal entitlement for his service in WW2. He was told that apart from the DFC he was entitled to 1939/45 Star, Air Europe Star, War Medal 1939/45, as well as the Air Efficiency Award for his service in the RAF Volunteer reserve. He was declined the Battle of Britain clasp, as this was awarded to flying personnel who flew in fighter aircraft of specific squadrons between 10th July 1940 and 31st October 1940. Ken was told his service with 219 squadron (night fighters) ceased on 29th June 1940. Ken did not challenge this, but his Log Book indicates he was on night fighters between July and October 1940. The author guesses he must have thought the word "specific" squadrons was the crucial statement.

Ken also asked about a Defence Medal covering the period between 3rd September 1939 and 8th May 1945, but was told that Prisoner of War Service does not count as qualifying for this medal.

CHAPTER 15

Summary

75TH ANNIVERSARY OF THE GREAT ESCAPE ON 24TH MARCH 1944.

I began this story stating that my father's life was extraordinary and I hope you will agree after reading this book! Remembering his age at the time (26 years old) having survived so many trips in his RAF career and being shot down - eventually surviving nearly two years of captivity in a cold barren camp, surrounded by fir trees and little else, his strength of character must have been resolute!

In March 2019, I had thc privilege of visiting the remains of

Stalag Luft 111 with my sister and my brother-in-law to see what is there. Little is left of the camp, but the foundations of buildings and the roadways can still be seen. The fire pits are still there and the remains of the washrooms, camp theatre, the underground hospital, and cooler floors are all still visible. The actual camp covers many different compounds - my father was in north compound, but there are east compound (from where the wooden horse escape happened), south compound and west compound as well as the Germans Lager (camp). At the time, the 75th Anniversary of the Great Escape was commemorated, and due honour was given to the 50 murdered aircrew by all nations involved. It was a very moving experience.

In early 1944, there were two other journalists in Stalag Luft 111 – Paul Brickhill and Conrad Norton, who realised that behind the monotonous routine lay some of the most fantastic incidents of the war and that the story of the camp must be told. They concluded that no camp in Germany held such a colourful and spectacular story, as north compound, Stalag Luft 111. They decided to record as much about the camp and its activities and they hid the evolving manuscript in hidey holes around the camp. During the "Long March" they carried all this paper on their backs. The whole manuscript was then published in 1946 via Faber & Faber. It was only produced in limited quantities however, as at the time there were considerable paper shortages. Ken told David Oldcorn that he was very uncomplimentary and bitter towards Paul Brickhill. This was because Brickhill insisted that he couldn't help carry anything other than the papers, with the intent of writing a book after the war – which he did. It was also known that Brickhill suffered from claustrophobia, so he didn't help with digging of any of the tunnels, which also was an annoyance to Ken.

I managed to get hold of a "Souvenir book" of Scangriff which was put together in the second half of 1945, by the Editorial staff (of which Ken was a member) of Scangriff, the newspaper of Stalag Luft 111. I felt certain extracts might be of interest to the readers and have been used in the writing of this book.

I also managed to track down a limited edition book called Sagan-the Log, published in August 1947, with the editor, Squadron Leader Bryce Cousens. It was due to be published in the summer of 1945 on return from Germany, but again, due to paper shortages, publication was delayed. It appears to have been sent to any ex POW from Stalag Luft 111, and a copy was sent to Ken. It seems that Bryce Cousens divided physical copies of their experiences with another officer, who unfortunately lost it on the "Long March" from Sagan in February 1945. He therefore recounts some experiences from his own memories. Cousens points out in the Foreword that the book was unpublished, not because of any supposed literary memories or historical merit, but purely as a reminder to us all of the joys, hopes, sorrows and disappointments which made up the days in Stalag Luft 111.

A mystery surrounds the fact that Cousens dedicated the book to the memory of those fifty-one (51) brother officers murdered by the Germans after escaping in 1944. However, every recount of this awful history related to Stalag Luft 111 and The Great Escape records the total to be fifty (50). He goes on to repeat this figure later in the manuscript, but is not in line with other published data, nor Hitler's instructions of fifty to be shot. This is also confirmed by the memorial to the murdered officers at Sagan. It may be that the effort of carrying these manuscripts home and the ordeal of the "Long March" may have had an effect – we shall never know.

In 1946, F/Lt Paul Brickhill and Conrad Norton published a more detailed book called "Escape to Danger", which included very much more than had been in the original Scandriff souvenir book and was on general sale at fifteen shillings. The author feels that reading this book, might help fully understand Ken's experiences. Being POWs in Stalag Luft 111, Brickhill's and Norton's comments and experiences are very much first hand.

About 10,000 men paid for their survival by dreary imprisonment behind barbed wire and the years they spent in those barren, cramped compounds were numb misery. It was such an indefinite purgatory. Life marked time, but despair and emotion didn't. They tried to escape. Brickhill & Norton started to write this book at the beginning of 1944 in Hut 103 (the tunnel Harry was in Hut 104). They hid the manuscript for a year from the Germans in wall panels or in the tunnel called Dick, which was never discovered by the Germans. They eventually lugged the manuscript on the refugee marches until the end of the war (each manuscript was reported to weigh 9.5 lbs). They say “Liberation” began to seem like a lovely dream, that would never come to pass.

A prisoner of war had to suffer the demoralising monotony of a life that did not vary one iota from day to day, for years. It was a life

SPOTLIGHT ON STALAG LUFT 3 BY SCANDRIFF SHOWING THE MEMORIAL IN 1945 UNDER THE HEADING “IN MEMORIAM”, UNDER WHICH KEN HAS WRITTEN IN INK

“Especially to my great friend and escaper Flt Lt Gordon P. Kidder (RCAF) shot by the gestapo in early April 1944. K G Price”

utterly devoid of any spot of colour or brightness, being just a drab existence that went from a ramshackle hut, to a small sandy desert of compound, enclosed by barbed wire, and back to the hut again. Consciousness and time became almost intolerable burdens, with no date to look forward to for release. Some POWs tried to commit suicide by gashing their wrists or rushing in frenzy at the barbed wire and being shot as soon as they crossed the warning area, which ran ten yards in from the fence.

Many who came home were badly affected by what they had endured and never spoke of the experience again, not wishing to relive the horrors they had gone through. The experiences of flying long range bombers through enemy territory; the terrors of being shot down, killed or horribly injured; the rigours or being locked up in a POW camp with all the deprivations that entailed, and the harsh conditions of the camp and the long march to freedom – all at the tender ages of between 20 to 30 years old. Then the return home to a country relieved to be at peace at long last, but showing remorse at the bombing campaign involved and not wishing to (until recently) show the gratitude that these men deserved for laying their lives on the line, night after night.

A very poignant reminder of the tragedy. Also shown is the Memorial in 2019, near the POW Camp in Sagan.

This is why I felt it was important to try to piece together my father's experience so that his life, his memory and what each of these people gave, can be saved for future generations. I hope you have found the story of my father's life interesting. He packed much into his relatively short life and is still greatly missed by his three children – Malcolm, Wendy & yours truly.

MEMORIAL NEAR SAGAN IN MARCH 2019

Further Reading which would add to this story:

Per Ardua Eagle

RAF Eagle scheme.

War and Pieces

Jack Lyon 2005

Stalag Luft 111 – the Secret Story

Arthur A Durand.

Lie in the dark and Listen

Wing Commander Ken Rees.

Looking into Hell – Experiences of the Bomber Command War

Mel Rolfe

Lancaster – the forging of a very British Legend

John Nichol

Spotlight on Stalag Luft 3

"Scangriff"

Sagan – The Log – published in August 1947